NCC
The National Computing Centre

The National Computing Centre develops techniques and provides aids for the more effective use of computers. NCC is a non-profit-distributing organisation backed by government and industry. The Centre

- co-operates with, and co-ordinates the work of, members and other organisations concerned with computers and their use

- provides information, advice and training

- supplies software packages

- publishes books

- promotes standards and codes of practice

Any interested company, organisation or individual can benefit from the work of the Centre by subscribing as a member. Throughout the country, facilities are provided for members to participate in working parties, study groups and discussions, and to influence NCC policy. A regular journal — 'NCC Interface' — keeps members informed of new developments and NCC activites. Special facilities are offered for courses, training material, publications and software packages.

For further details get in touch with the Centre at Oxford Road, Manchester M1 7ED (telephone 061-228 6333)

or at one of the following regional offices

Belfast	1st Floor	Glasgow	2nd Floor,
	117 Lisburn Road		Anderston House
	BT9 7BP		Argyle Street
Telephone:	0232 665997		G2 8LR
		Telephone:	041-204 1101
Birmingham	2nd Floor		
	Prudential Buildings	London	11 New Fetter Lane
	Colmore Row		EC4A 1PU
	B3 2PL	Telephone:	01-353 4875
Telephone:	021-236 6283		
Bristol	6th Floor		
	Royal Exchange Building		
	41 Corn Street		
	BS1 1HG		
Telephone:	0272 27077		

COMPUTERS AND THE PROFESSIONAL

Elements of BASIC

by

R. LEWIS, MSc MBCS
Lecturer in Education, Chelsea College, University of London

and

B. H. BLAKELEY, BSc AFIMA
Head of Applied Mathematics, Highgate School

Editor: J. J. Turnbull BSc
Senior Consultant, NCC

PUBLISHED BY NCC PUBLICATIONS

Keywords for information retrieval drawn
from *NCC Thesaurus of Computing Terms:*
BASIC (language), Exercises

1st Edition, 1972
2nd Edition, 1974
2nd Impression 1974
Reprinted 1980

ISBN 0 85012 118 3

Reprinted Offset Litho by Wright's (Sandbach) Limited
9 Middlewich Road, Sandbach, Cheshire

Contents

Introduction

The programming language known as BASIC (a mnemonic for Beginner's All-purpose Symbolic Instruction Code) was designed at Dartmouth College in the United States for use in an educational environment. Originally BASIC was used principally for numerical work, but its content has been expanded and its area of application broadened beyond educational use. The introduction of string and file handling has made it an appropriate language for a wider class of problems in data processing, and current applications include computer aided instruction, text analysis and simulation. Although BASIC was designed as an educational language, the simplicity of its syntax has made it very popular with the writer of occasional programs in industry and commerce and in universities and other research establishments. BASIC is now a major language offered by time-sharing companies and versions of BASIC are available on most mini-computers.

This text introduces BASIC through a series of problems which gradually develop the full power of the language. The various components of the language are introduced as they become *useful* in solving the problems being considered. As far as possible the text is machine independent and is independent of the type of access to the computer being used. However, the user of a small mini-computer may be restricted to a mathematical sub-set of BASIC and so will not be able to implement all the ideas of Chapters 3, 7 and 8. The users of a batch processing system will find it necessary to study the details of the READ and DATA statements in Chapter 3, using this method of input of data rather than the INPUT statement described in Chapter 1.

The machine independent approach cannot be maintained when file handling is considered. Consequently chapter 7 covers the general principles of file handling and reference to particular systems is made by means of loose cards inserted in the back cover of the book. These cards cover most of the available major interactive implementations of the language. Computer companies have also developed other features of the language which may be peculiar to their particular system. These features are not essential to a general understanding of BASIC though they may be extremely useful in certain applications. For these features the user is referred to the manufacturers' handbooks.

In the preparation of this book a great deal of attention has been given to its design so that it can be used as part of a course in computing at secondary school level. It deals only with programming, a small but necessary part in a course of computer appreciation, but many of the problems discussed allow an easy expansion to wider considerations of problem solving, model building, the application of computers in business, society and science and to the social implications of the use of computers.

In schools, teachers may find that the first four chapters can form the basis of a course for 13–16 year olds. It is certainly possible to teach computer studies with little reference to, or need of, mathematics. This is possible if selected parts of the work are chosen and in fact, the book has been written with this idea in mind. For the non-mathematical approach, the following sequence may be tried:
Chapters 1, 3, 4, 6, 7 with the addition of parts of 2 if, and when, these prove useful.

A programming language is written to be used, not to provide exercises in its own right. Learning a programming language is not, in itself, a particularly valuable logical exercise, although it can prove to be a valuable accompaniment to flow-charting and the basic ideas of problem-solving; further, great depth of programming experience is not necessary for an appreciation of the significance of the computer. The purpose of this book, therefore, is to provide a tool which it is hoped will add a new dimension to the reader's particular area of application.

Acknowledgement

The National Computing Centre and the authors wish to thank the staff and students of a number of organisations for their help in the development of this book. They also acknowledge the help by the Computer industry in preparing the Card Supplements.

Introducing BASIC

Flowcharts

This book is going to assume that you have a reasonable knowledge of flow-charts such as the one on the right. By convention, different shapes of box are used to indicate various operations.

For example:

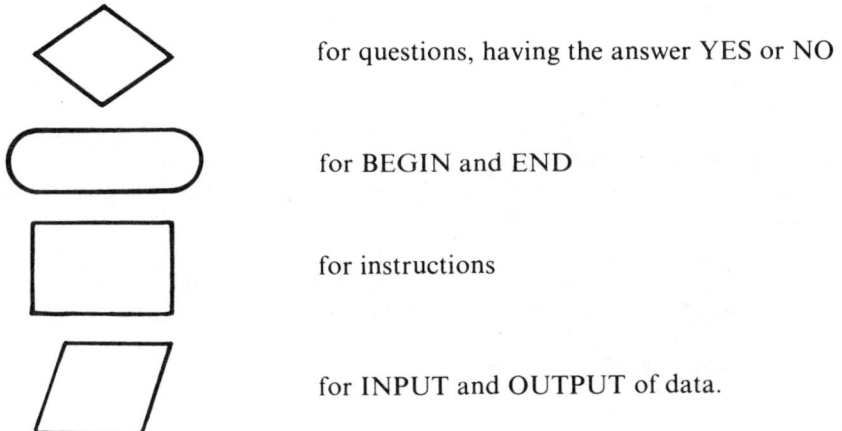

for questions, having the answer YES or NO

for BEGIN and END

for instructions

for INPUT and OUTPUT of data.

One or two other symbols will be introduced as there is a need for them.

Flowcharts provide us with an excellent way in which to set out a series of instructions which must be obeyed in a particular order and some of which may have to be obeyed more than once. If we wish to solve a problem, we need to produce such a series of instructions; we can then present these instructions to another person, who, by following them, can also obtain a solution to the problem.

If we want a computer to solve a problem for us we have to prepare a series of instructions, which the computer will accept and act upon. We provide the logical structure of the solution and the computer simply obeys our instructions, performing the necessary operations as defined by these instructions. This series of instructions is known as a program.

Flowchart to arrange
two words in alphabetic order

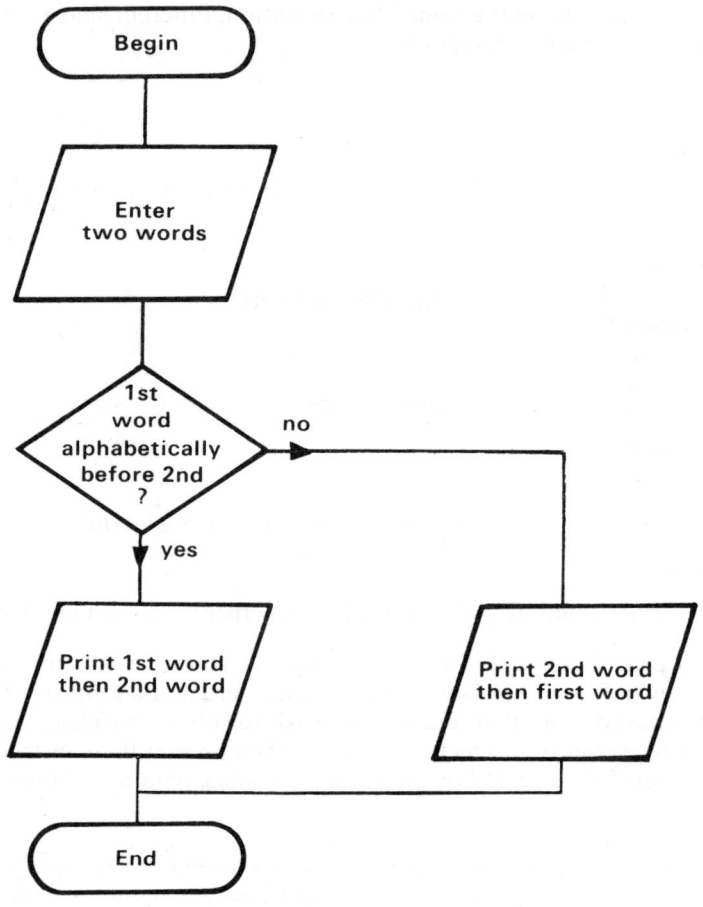

The computer

A computer can be thought of as being made up of five units:

the INPUT UNIT — so that we can get instructions and data into the computer

the OUTPUT UNIT — so that we can get information out of the computer

the ARITHMETIC UNIT — where the computer can perform the necessary additions, subtractions, multiplications, divisions and comparisons, using data from the store

the STORE — in which are held instructions, raw data and calculated data

the CONTROL UNIT — which ensures that each of the other units is brought into play at the appropriate time, according to instructions held in the store or given directly by the computer operator.

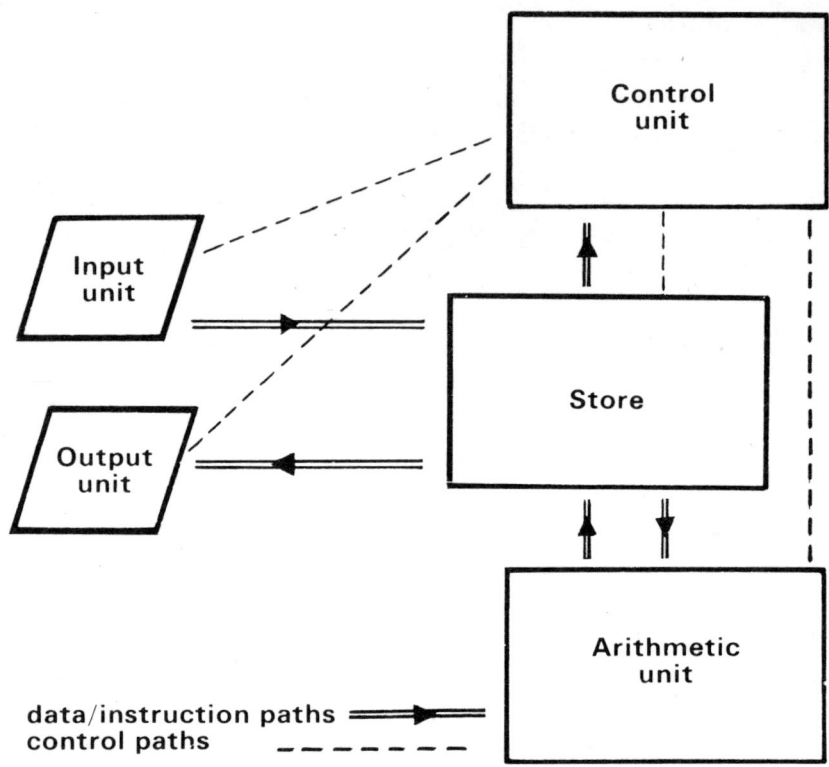

There are many methods of input, but in this book we shall be mainly concerned with the teleprinter terminal, which also acts as the output unit.

The store will hold not only the data for our particular problem and the calculated results, but also the instructions which enable the computer to solve the problem. Before the computer can start work on the problem, the data and the instructions must be placed in particular locations within the store, which have addresses (like individual houses in a town have addresses), so that reference can be made to them as is necessary. As a simplification we shall think of the store as being divided into two parts. That part which holds the data will be addressed by letters and that part which holds the instructions will be addressed by numbers. There is no actual distinction within the store, but this idea will be found helpful. Each letter will be the reference (or ADDRESS) of one item of data, and each number will be the reference (or ADDRESS) of one instruction.

The program

The STATEMENTS (or instructions) of the language BASIC which make up the program are very simple. Many problems can be solved by using only a small range of statements:

INPUT A takes an item of data from the input device and stores this in location A, overwriting anything that is already in location A

PRINT A takes a copy of the contents of location A and prints it on the output device

LET $A = B + C$ copies of the contents of locations B and C are taken to the arithmetic unit where they are added and the result stored in location A

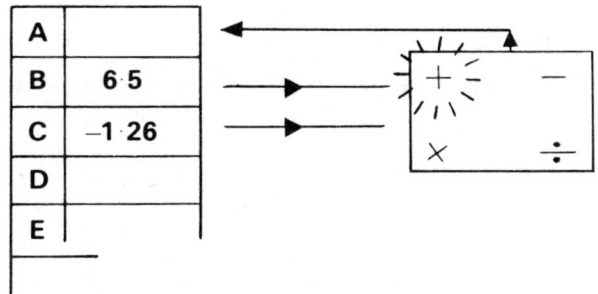

LET $A = B - C$

LET $A = B * C$ *is the symbol for multiplication

LET $A = B/C$ / is the symbol for division

END   appears as the final statement in any program and tells the computer to stop working on that program

It is also possible to have statements of the form

LET $A = A + 2$ a copy of the contents of location A is taken to the arith-
                       metic unit where 2 is added to it and the result stored
                       back in location A, thereby overwriting the original
                       contents of A.

                       Notice that '2' is not contained in a storage location but
                       is generated by the computer when required.

LET $B = A + 2.75$

LET $X = -2.5/Y$ Numbers may be introduced in any statements. They
                       may be positive or negative and may be decimal as
                       shown.

LET $C = 3.14 * D$

LET $P = 16/25$

Now let us see how some of these statements can be put together to tackle a
particular problem.

Problem

Convert a sum of money in pounds and pence into dollars and cents, given that
the conversion rate is 2·39 dollars to the pound.

This is, of course, a very simple problem for which it is not really worth writing
a program, but it demonstrates the structure of most problems. To solve the
problem we shall have to input some data (the amount of money in pounds and
pence) we shall have to process this data (i.e. actually do the arithmetic involved
in the conversion) and we shall expect some new data to be output (the corresponding amount of money in dollars and cents).

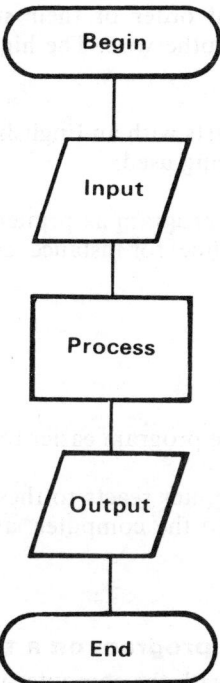

If we use S to refer to the amount of money in £ p, and D to refer to the amount in dollars and cents, it is easy to see that the following statements are necessary to accomplish the task –

```
1 INPUT S
2 LET D = 2·39*S
3 PRINT D
4 END
```

Note that we have not included a 'BEGIN' instruction. Such an instruction is not included in the program as fed into the computer, but is given directly to the control unit after all the statements have been fed in.

1, 2, 3 and 4 are called statement numbers and each statement must have a number. The first statement does not have to be number 1, nor do the successive statement numbers have to increase in units of 1. In fact, using 10, 20, 30, etc. will allow us to insert a statement in between two earlier statements without having to change all the statement numbers. The computer will deal with statements in the numerical order of their statement numbers unless it is instructed specifically to do otherwise. The highest numbered statement must be the END statement.

Note that each statement starts with an English word which tells the computer what kind of statement is being used.

It is not apparent from the program as printed, but spaces have no meaning in the statements. The third line, for instance, could well have been

   3PRINTD

and the second line

   2LET$D = 2\cdot39*S$

We insert spaces to make the program easier to read.

Before we see how the computer reacts to these statements, we must first see how to get the program into the computer, and this involves the use of the teleprinter terminal.

Entering and running a program on a terminal

Establishing initial contact with the computer will vary from system to system and this may involve naming the program. The processes required by some systems are dealt with in Chapter 7. We shall assume that contact has been made with the computer and the computer is ready for you to enter your program. This will be indicated by the computer printing out, at the terminal some word such as READY. The user then types out each line of the program, including the line number. At the end of each line, the user must strike the carriage return key – this indicates to the computer that the current line is complete (we shall use cr. to denote the use of the carriage return key). Some systems require the use of some other key to terminate a line, reference should be made to the manufacturer's manual.

In some systems, if an error has been made in a line, such as typing

   10 INPUR S

there will be an immediate indication with the printing of an error message on the terminal. In other systems, these error messages are held until an attempt is made to run the program. If the user realises he has made a mistake in a line, he can correct it simply by keying cr., and then retyping the line number and line.

When the typing in of the program is complete, the program will be held in a certain part of the computer store and there it will stay, without anything happening, until the instruction to start running the program is given. As noted before, this instruction is not included in the program. To get the computer to run the program the user types RUN cr. RUN is one of a number of SYSTEM COMMANDS which are acted upon immediately to control the operation of the computer system.

At this stage the computer will complete its checks of the input program to see that no invalid statements have been typed. If the error messages have not already been printed they will now be output at the terminal, and if there are none, the program, having been changed into the computer's internal code, will be executed.

In the program above, the first statement the computer meets is the input statement. Its response is to print a '?' at the terminal and then wait for the user to type in the value of S (the number of £ p which is to be converted) – say 12·75 – followed by cr. The carriage return indicates that the input is complete and the 12·75 is stored in a location 'S'. The computer then automatically proceeds to the next statement. The second statement refers to 'S' so the computer looks in its store to find location S. Having found the 12·75 which it placed there during the first instruction the computer takes a copy of this number to the arithmetic unit, generates the number 2·39 referred to in the instruction, multiplies these numbers in the arithmetic unit and places the result in location D in the store. Location D now holds the number 30·4725, and the computer proceeds to the next statement. The third statement refers to 'D' so the computer looks in its store for location D, finds the 30·4725 placed there during the last statement, and takes a copy and prints it at the terminal as instructed. The computer then proceeds to the next statement and ENDs.

If we wish to convert another sum of money we must again type RUN cr, respond to the '?' with the sum to be converted, and the result will again be printed out at the terminal.

Before we proceed to some problems for you to try, it may be useful to give one or two tips on using the teleprinter terminal. The problems may seem very easy, but it is wise at this stage not to try to rush ahead. Experience must be gained in the entering and running of programs and now is the time to gain it.

We have already mentioned the possibility of typing a line wrongly, put right by typing cr. and retyping the complete line. The computer will replace the first copy of the line with the second copy. An alternative procedure is to delete the wrong character typed by typing ← or some such character (this will be determined by the particular system or teleprinter being used) and following this with the correct character.

Thus the line

    10 INPUR←T A cr.

will be taken by the computer to be

    10 INPUT A

It is possible to use this character a number of times in succession to delete a number of characters, working back from the current position of the typing head. Thus:

    10 LET←←·←INPUT A cr.

is equivalent to typing

    10 INPUT A cr.

If you find that you wish to erase a statement entirely, type the statement number and follow it by cr. The computer simply removes the original statement with that number.

If you find that you have omitted a statement you may type it at any stage before typing the command RUN, even after the END statement. The END statement must be the highest numbered statement in a program but the order of typing in the statements is not important. The computer will sort out the statements into the correct order after the RUN command. The following program will run quite satisfactorily –

    10 LET $D = 2·39 * S$
    20 END
    15 PRINT D
     5 INPUT S

Notice how giving the PRINT statement a statement number of 15 will make sure that it is obeyed between statements 10 and 20.

Problems 1A

Investigate the computer's response to the following sets of instructions:

```
1A.1  10 INPUT X
      20 LET Y = X*X
      30 PRINT X
      40 PRINT Y
      50 END
```

```
1A.2  10 INPUT X
      30 LET Z = X + Y
      20 INPUT Y
      40 PRINT X, Y, Z
      50 END
```

```
1A.3  10 INPUT X
      20 LET A = X + Y
      30 PRINT A
      40 END
```

```
1A.4  10 INPUT X
      20 LET Y = X − X
      30 PRINT X, Y
      40 LET B = 2/Y
      50 PRINT B
      60 END
```

1A.5 Taxi fares are calculated by adding to a standing charge of 15p a charge of 3p per half mile for every mile over two. Input the length of a journey (in complete miles) and output the length and the cost.

1A.6 Write a program which calculates the area of a circle when you have input the radius, and prints out the radius and the area.

1A.7 Write a program which converts a distance in yards (to be input) into metres, printing out both forms of the distance. Do this for three or four distances.

Input and output of data

It should be stated that these problems did not make good use of the computer. In fact it would probably have been quicker to have done the calculations by hand! Let us try to improve on that. In fact let us make our introductory program on currency conversion deal with conversion from sterling into any currency. This means that instead of multiplying by 2·39 we shall multiply by R where R is the rate of exchange concerned, and this will have to be input at the start of the program. The program might now be –

```
10 INPUT S
20 INPUT R
30 LET D = S*R
40 PRINT S
50 PRINT D
60 END
```

To avoid having two input and output statements we can use:

```
10 INPUT S, R
```

and 40 PRINT S, D

and omit lines 20 and 50. When the program is run, line 10 will produce the '?' from the computer which should be answered by the values of S and R (in that order) separated by a comma. Line 40 will produce the values of S and D on one line, spaced so as to accommodate five numbers to one line of type.

It would be pleasant, at this stage, to be able to print out some words as headings or indications of what the numbers printed are. This is very simple, as shown in the program and printout on the right; the required words being enclosed within quotation marks in a PRINT statement. More extensive use of text and control over the format of output is covered in Chapter 3.

A program title (CONVER in this case) is required on most systems. Details of naming a program are given in Chapter 7 or reference may be made to the manual describing a particular system.

```
LIST
CONVER

5   PRINT "CURRENCY CONVERSION"
10    INPUT S,R
20    LET D=S*R
30    PRINT "POUNDS        EQUIVALENT"
40    PRINT S,D
50    END


RUN
CONVER   1016

CURRENCY CONVERSION
?12.50,2.40
POUNDS         EQUIVALENT
 12.5               30

DONE AT 1016


RUN
CONVER   1016

CURRENCY CONVERSION
?25.72,2.41
POUNDS         EQUIVALENT
 25.72           61.9852

DONE AT 1016
```

Problems 1B

1B.1 Calculate the square and cube of a number. Print out the number, its square and its cube.

1B.2 Calculate the volume of a circular cylinder, having first input the radius and height. Output the radius, height and volume under headings of RADIUS, HEIGHT, VOLUME.

1B.3 Calculate the simple interest on a given sum of money (P) for a given time (T) at a given rate of interest (R). The sum (in pounds), the time (in years) and the rate (in % per year) should be fed in. Title and head your output.

1B.4 Convert a given number of days, hours and minutes into minutes.

1B.5 Calculate the income tax on a sum of money greater than £500 (to be input) assuming a single man's allowance of £350 and tax at the rate of 38·25% on the remainder. Output the gross and nett incomes.

1B.6 In the calculation of income tax, there are many more factors than those of problem 1B.5. Find out the current rates and details for a single person and extend your previous program to include some of these factors. Output, as appropriate, under suitable headings.

Simple jump statements

Now is the time for us to make our programs more ambitious, and to get a little nearer to using the true power of the computer. In our previous program for currency conversion –

```
10 INPUT S, R
30 LET D = S*R
40 PRINT S, D
60 END
```

It would be sensible to use the same program for the conversion of a number of different sums of money from sterling into dollars. In other words we should like the program, having obeyed statement 40, not to stop, but to return automatically to do another calculation. This is possible using a new type of statement – a GOTO statement. It is of the form GOTO n, where n is a statement number occurring in the program. Our first attempt at using this statement might be as in the flowchart and program on the right.

Two points to note are:

i) the way in which input statements have been separated, so as to avoid having to enter the conversion rate every time a new sum of money is input.

ii) The necessity for the END statement. Without this the computer would send an error message.

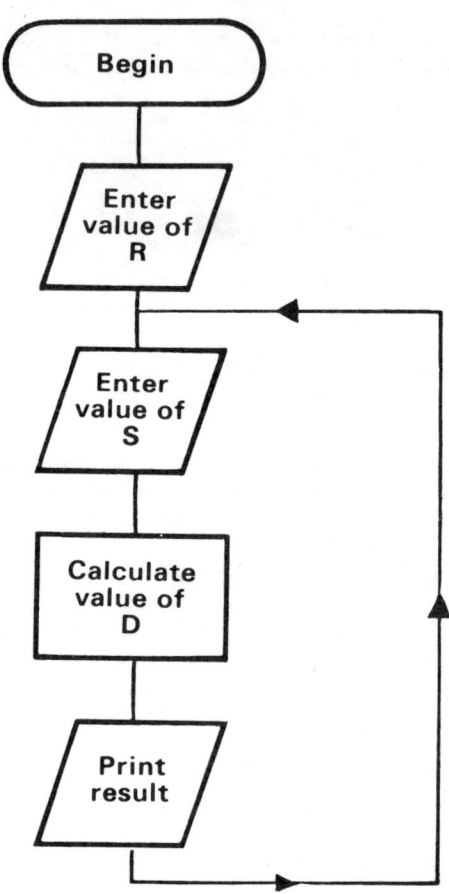

```
10 INPUT R
20 INPUT S
30 LET D=S*R
40 PRINT S,D
50 GOTO 20
60 END
```

There is an important fault in the program however – we have no way of making the program end when we want it to. After entering the last piece of data that we wish to convert, the computer will do the calculation, print out the result, go to line 20, and print a '?' waiting for more data. To get over this problem we shall arrange to signal to the computer, when we have finished entering data, by putting in a false piece of data. In this case a zero would do very well.

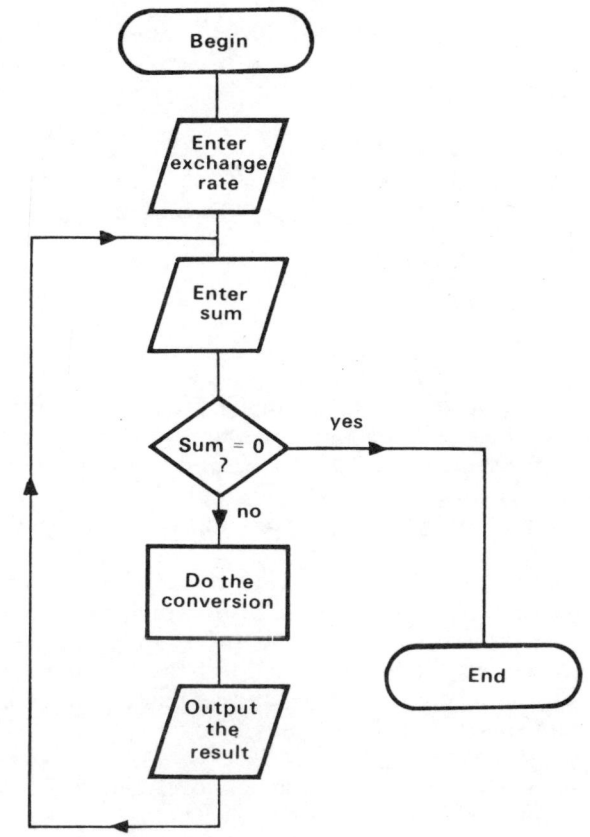

Each time a piece of data has been input we arrange for the program to see if it is the zero which marks the end of the data, and, if so, to jump to the end of the program. If the data input is not the zero, we shall wish the program to continue and do the conversion.

To allow the computer to decide whether to do the conversion, or to end the program, we make use of a new statement, often referred to as a conditional jump. This takes the form

IF $A = B$ THEN n

where A and B are numbers calculated in the program (normally referred to as variables), or constants, and where n is a statement number.

The program for the flowchart on the left would be:

```
10 INPUT R
20 INPUT S
30 IF S=0 THEN 100
40 LET D=S*R
45 PRINT "POUNDS            DOLLARS"
50 PRINT S,D
60 GOTO 20
100 END
```

Notice that in this program the computer does not take the statements always in the order of their line numbers. Each time until the final input the lines will be obeyed in the order 10, 20, 30, 40 (because the value input for S will not be zero), 50, 60 and then not 100 but 20 again. On the last input, statement 30 would be followed by 100 because the input value of S would be zero.

Now that the programs are getting a little longer you may well be making a few alterations as you type the program in. It would be useful to have a correct version of the program and this is possible by typing the system command LIST, followed by cr. The computer will then print out at the terminal a complete copy of the program as it stands at that time, with all the lines in their correct order. This can be done at any time.

The system command SCRATCH will remove completely the current program from the computer store.

It is important to understand the difference between statements and system commands. Statements are stored in the computer at specific addresses (their statement number) and are quite inactive until the program of which they are a part is executed. On the other hand, system commands are acted upon immediately they are received by the computer and so do not need to be stored.

The ideas covered can be seen in a typical printout, for a program called CONV2, from a session at a terminal.

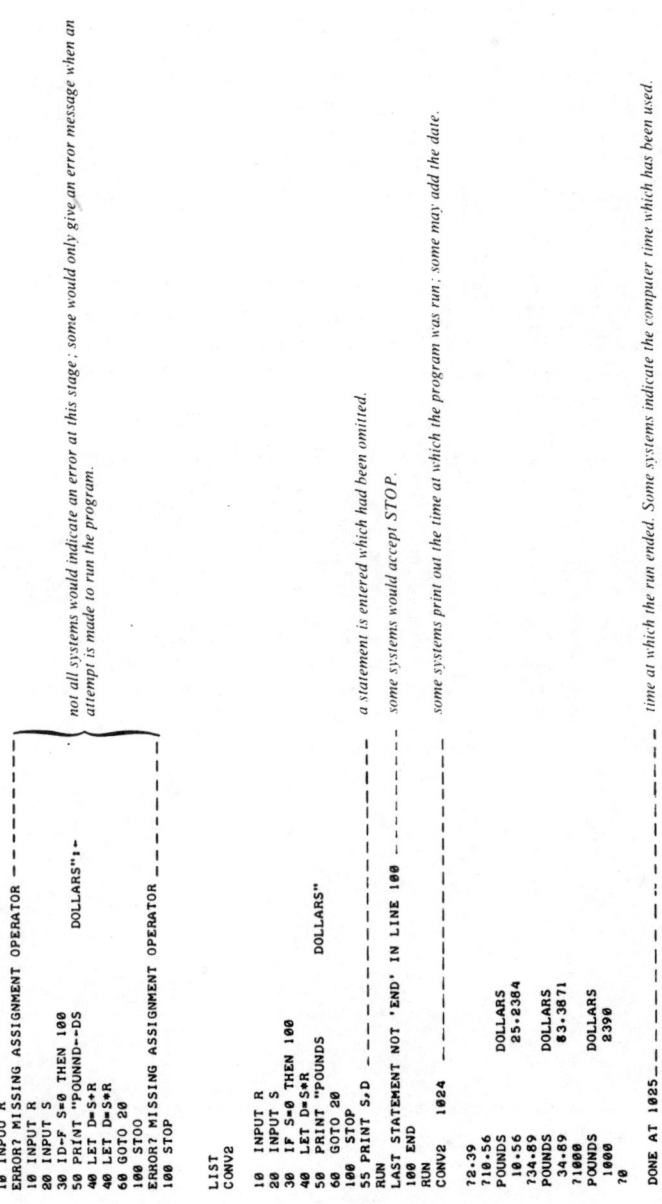

```
10 INPUU R
ERROR? MISSING ASSIGNMENT OPERATOR  - - - - - -
10 INPUT R
20 INPUT S
30 ID-F S=0 THEN 100
50 PRINT "POUNND--DS        DOLLARS"!-
40 LET D=S*R
40 LET D=S*R
60 GOTO 20
100 STOO
ERROR? MISSING ASSIGNMENT OPERATOR  - - - - - -
100 STOP

LIST
CONV2
10  INPUT R
20  INPUT S
30  IF S=0 THEN 100
40  LET D=S*R
50  PRINT "POUNDS        DOLLARS"
60  GOTO 20
100 STOP
55 PRINT S,D  - - - - - - - - - - - - - - - - -
RUN
LAST STATEMENT NOT 'END' IN LINE 100  - - - - - -
100 END
RUN
CONV2    1024  - - - - - - - - - - - - - - - - -

72.39
710.56
POUNDS        DOLLARS
10.56         25.2384
734.89
POUNDS        DOLLARS
34.89         83.3871
71000
POUNDS        DOLLARS
1000          2390
70

DONE AT 1025  - - - - - - - - - - - - - - - - -
```

not all systems would indicate an error at this stage : some would only give an error message when an attempt is made to run the program.

a statement is entered which had been omitted.

some systems would accept STOP.

some systems print out the time at which the program was run : some may add the date.

time at which the run ended. Some systems indicate the computer time which has been used.

Problems 1C

1C.1 Convert a number of measurements in feet and inches into metres. (Adapt your program for 1B.1). Output your results in columns headed FEET, INCHES and METRES.

1C.2 Adapt your program for 1B.2 to investigate how the volume of a cylinder varies with the radius (keeping the height constant). Then investigate how the volume varies with the height.

1C.3 Produce a table of the squares and cubes of the integers from 1 to 10 inclusive.

1C.4 A salesman's record slip consists of a customer identification number, the number of articles bought, the price and discount rate for that customer (say, 10%, 20% etc.). Prepare an invoice showing (with appropriate headings) the customer number, the number of articles bought, the discount and the amount due.

1C.5 Input the lengths of the three sides of a triangle and test to see if it is a right-angled triangle.

1C.6 Write a program which accepts a whole number as input and tests to see if it is an even or odd number.

1C.7 Write a program which accepts, as input, firstly an amount of money placed in a bank account, then a number of sums of money which may be withdrawn from the account (negative sums) or paid into the account (positive sums). When the amount zero is input the program should print out the current state of the account.

Summary of the main points from Chapter One

Chapter One has introduced some BASIC statements and shown how these can be arranged to form a program.

The statements used include:

$$\begin{array}{lll}
\text{INPUT } A & \text{or} & \text{INPUT } A, B, C \\
\text{PRINT } A & \text{or} & \text{PRINT } A, B, C \\
\text{LET } A = B + C & \text{or} & \text{LET } A = A + 2{\cdot}1 \\
\text{LET } A = B - C & \text{or} & \text{LET } A = A - 4 \\
\text{LET } A = B*C & \text{or} & \text{LET } A = 2{\cdot}6*B \\
\end{array}$$

* is the symbol for multiplication

$$\text{LET } A = B/C \qquad \text{or} \qquad \text{LET } A = 1{\cdot}2/C$$

/ is the symbol for division

GOTO n

IF $A = B$ THEN n or IF $A = 0$ THEN n where n is a statement number

PRINT "ANY TEXT INCLUDING SPACES"

END

Each statement has a statement number, the highest being the number of the END statement.

Chapter 2

Extending BASIC Statements

Assignment statements

So far we have used statements which assign to the variable on the left-hand side the value of simple expressions which involve only two variables, such as in LET $A = B+C$, or a variable and a constant such as in LET $A = B+4\cdot1$. In the normal use of algebra we have much more complicated expressions and BASIC can cope with expressions such as:

$$x = \frac{a+b}{2} \text{ or } C = \frac{5}{9}(F-32) \text{ or even } y = \frac{1}{5}(a+b+c+d+e)$$

the corresponding statements in BASIC being:

LET $X = (A+B)/2$
LET $C = 5/9*(F-32)$ and
LET $Y = 1/5*(A+B+C+D+E)$

When using statements like these, the only requirement is that all of the variables on the **right-hand side** of the statement must have working values, that is to say that a value must have previously been input for them during the program, or a value must previously have been calculated for them in the program.

The function of brackets in a statement is precisely that of brackets in an algebraic expression, i.e. to indicate an order of evaluation. For instance, in the first of the above expressions

LET $X = (A+B)/2$

the computer will take copies of the contents of locations A and B into the arithmetic unit, where they will be added, and the result held until the computer has produced a '2', when the sum will be divided by 2 and the result placed in location X. If we omit the brackets however –

LET $X = A+B/2$

the computer will first take a copy of the contents of location B into the arithmetic unit, divide it by 2 and hold the result until a copy of the contents of location A has been obtained. This will be added to the result of the division, the final result being placed in location X.

So we can see that the computer has a certain order in which it will perform operations. Just as in algebra, expressions in brackets are evaluated first, then multiplication and division is carried out and finally addition and subtraction. The rules for writing expressions are identical to the rules for ordinary algebra.

There is also one additional operation which was not in the introductory list in chapter one – that of raising to a power. The statements

LET $Y = B*B$ and LET $Y = B \uparrow 2$

are equivalent, the vertical arrow meaning 'raised to the power'. The power itself may be a variable, as in

LET $Y = B \uparrow C$

or an expression as in

LET $Y = B \uparrow (C + D)$.

The order of performing operations on the computer is:

  i) all calculations within brackets
 ii) $\uparrow$
iii) * and /
 iv) + and − .

This is fine until we come to a statement such as

LET $A = B*D/C$

where both the * and the / rank equally in the order of operations. In this case the expression is scanned from left to right and the operations performed as they are encountered, i.e. in the example given, the multiplication is carried out first and the result is then divided by C. Note, however, that in the statement

LET $A = B + D/C$

the division would be performed first because division precedes addition in the order of operations. If it is desired that the sum of B and D be found first, the statement must be written

LET $A = (B + D)/C$

The reader should be prepared to experiment with expressions like these, giving simple values to the variables involved and checking his results with those given by the computer. It may be helpful to compare the following algebraic expressions with their corresponding BASIC statements.

$$a = \frac{b+c+d}{3} \qquad \text{LET } A = (B+C+D)/3$$

$$y = 3x^2 + 2x \qquad \text{LET } Y = 3*X \uparrow 2 + 2*X$$

$$v = \frac{4}{3}\pi r^3 \qquad \text{LET } V = 4/3*P*R \uparrow 3$$

P must previously have been given the appropriate value

$$g = \frac{a-b}{s-y} \qquad \text{LET } G = (A-B)/(S-Y)$$

$$s = ut + \tfrac{1}{2}at^2 \qquad \text{LET } S = U*T + 1/2*A*T \uparrow 2$$

It is most important to realise that the 'equals' sign in an algebraic expression and the 'equals' sign in a program statement mean completely different things. In algebra ' = ' simply means that the two expressions on either side have the same value, but in a program statement the ' = ' is an instruction to the computer to take the expression on the right-hand side, calculate its value, and place the result in the storage location named on the left-hand side. Thus, although the expression

$$a + b = c + d$$

is perfectly valid in algebra, the statement

LET $A + B = C + D$

is quite meaningless and will be greeted with an error message if it is included in a program.

The reader should realise that in a complex statement such as

LET $Y = 3*X \uparrow 3 - 4*X \uparrow 2 + 6*X - 7$

there are a number of intermediate results, all of which are allocated storage space by the computer until such time as they are required. Firstly the $X \uparrow 3$ and the $X \uparrow 2$ are calculated and stored, then the $3*X \uparrow 3$, $4*X \uparrow 2$ and $6*X$ are calculated and stored, and finally the $4*X \uparrow 2$ is subtracted from the $3*X \uparrow 3$, the $6*X$ is added to the result and 7 is subtracted from that result, the final result being stored in location Y.

Problems 2A

2A.1 Calculate the value of $y = 2x^3 - 6x^2 + 15x - 21$ for any value of x (to be input). Use this program to help you to draw the graph of

$$y = 2x^3 - 6x^2 + 15x - 21.$$

2A.2 Write a program which will convert degrees Centigrade into degrees Fahrenheit. Can you extend this program to accept the input of a temperature either in °C or °F and then to carry out the appropriate conversion?

2A.3 If money is invested and, at the end of each year the interest is not taken out but added to the investment ('compound interest') the formula

$$A = P\left(1 + \frac{r}{100}\right)^n$$

gives the amount (A) to which an investment (P) will grow, after n years at $r\%$ per year. Compare the amounts, after various times, for the same amount invested at compound interest and simple interest (see problem 1B.3).

2A.4 Investigate, for various numbers, the ways of raising to a power a number raised to a power. In other words, is

$$\left(n^n\right)^n \text{ the same as } n^{\left(n^n\right)} \text{?}$$

Is one expression always bigger than the other? Is there a range of numbers for which one expression is always the larger? Extend your investigation to the case of three powers – i.e.

$$\left(n^{n^n}\right)^n, \; \left(n^n\right)^{\left(n^n\right)}, \; n^{\left(n^{n^n}\right)} \text{ etc.}$$

2A.5 Write a program to accept, as input, a set of marks, and to calculate the average of the set.

2A.6 Write a program to produce batting averages – that is a listing of number of innings, number of times 'not out', number of runs scored, average runs scored. The input for any innings should indicate whether out or not as well as the number of runs scored. It is normal practice to give an average only after a batsman has been 'out' at least once – why?

Conditional jump statements

We have already used a conditional jump instruction where the jump is dependent on two variables being equal, or on one variable being equal to a certain value, e.g.

IF $A = B$ THEN 50   or   IF $A = 10$ THEN 100

In these 'IF' statements, we can also have other conditions in place of the equality:

$<$ (less than)
$>$ (greater than)
$< =$ (less than or equal to)
$> =$ (greater than or equal to)
$< >$ (less than or greater than, i.e. not equal to)

Remember that, in a statement such as

IF $A = B$ THEN 120

if the condition is satisfied the program jumps to obey statement number 120, and if the condition is not satisfied the program continues with the statement immediately following the IF statement.

Suppose we wish to find out, for various sums invested at compound interest, how long it takes for the amount to reach £1000. One way would be to run the program on the right and when the printout shows an amount greater than £1000 to stop the program and run it again for the next sum of money, and so on.

This method of tackling the problem brings one or two difficulties – even though we do not have an 'END' in the flowchart we must have an 'END' statement in the program or else the computer will not accept the program. When we type RUN cr. the computer will start to print out the required values at the teleprinter and will go on printing! How do we stop a program when it has started running? The precise method will depend on the system being used, but will probably consist of depressing the 'BREAK' key or some other key on the teleprinter.

A flowchart, program and two typical runs follow.

Flowchart for
program COMINT

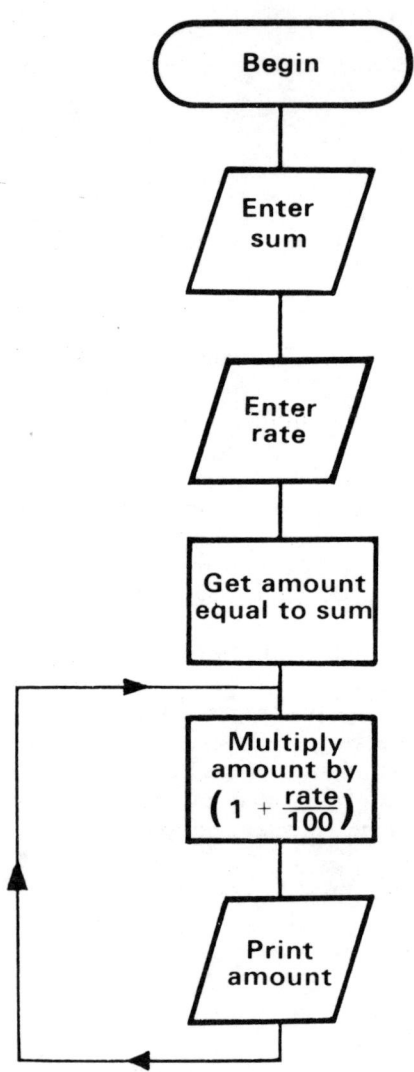

```
LIST

COMINT

10    INPUT S
20    INPUT R
30    LET A=S
40    LET A=A*(1+R/100)
50    PRINT A
60    GOTO 40
70    END



RUN
COMINT   1030

?750
?8
 810
 874.8
 944.784
 1020.37
 1102.
 1
STOP
RUN
COMINT   1030

?750
?5
 787.5
 826.875
 868.219
 911.63
 957.211
 1005.07
 1055.32
STOP
```

We now have to count up the number of lines printed until £1000 is reached and we have the answer to our question. If we try to improve the program – and it is not a recommended procedure to put an infinite loop in a program – it is quite easy to see that the addition of the statement

55 IF $A = 1000$ THEN 70

Would do no good at all, because the amount will probably not be exactly equal to 1000. The condition would not be satisfied, and the program would not jump to 'END'. The statement required is

55 IF $A > = 1000$ THEN 70

It is good practice to use $> =$ in IF statements rather than $=$ to guard against the possibility of an infinite loop if the 'equals' condition is not exactly satisfied.

The program could be further improved by providing a means of counting the number of times the program goes round the loop, and making the only printout the value of this 'counter' together with the amount when the £1000 is exceeded or equalled. The program, COMIN2, which follows also shows an alternative way of dealing with the exit from the loop.

```
LIST
COMIN2

10   INPUT S
20   INPUT R
25   LET C=0
30   LET A=S
40   LET A=A*(1+R/100)
45   LET C=C+1
50   IF A<1000 THEN 40
55   PRINT "AFTER ";C;" YEARS THE AMOUNT WILL BE #";A
60   END


RUN
COMIN2   1039

?750
?5
AFTER   6       YEARS THE AMOUNT WILL BE #  1005.07

DONE AT 1039
```

Similar methods can be used to solve the problem:

> Starting at 1, and adding up all the whole numbers, that is $1+2+3+\ldots$ etc., how far do we have to go before the sum is greater than 100? How far before the sum is greater than 1000?

We shall arrange to have a running total which will be increased by a number which itself increases by 1 each time we go round a loop. Each time the running total has been increased, we shall check to see if it has reached, or passed the limit we have set. The flowchart, which follows, summarises the process. This is then used in the program SUMINT.

Flowchart for program SUMINT

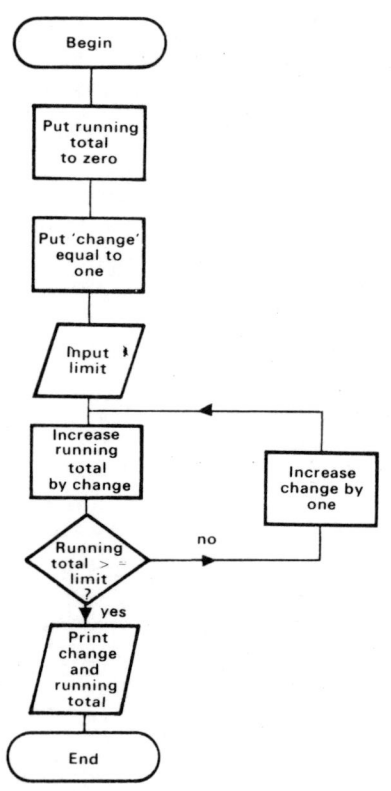

```
LIST
SUMINT

10   LET  S=0
20   LET  C=1
30   INPUT  L
40   LET  S=S+C
50   IF  S  >= L  THEN 80
60   LET  C=C+1
70   GOTO  40
80   PRINT  C,S
90   END


RUN
SUMINT   1044

?200
 20              210

DONE AT 1044
```

Simple sorting

Now that the IF statement is available, we are able to tackle the problem of using the computer to arrange numbers in order. The flowchart and program (ORDER) which follow show the simplest case of arranging two numbers in ascending order.

```
LIST
ORDER

10   INPUT A,B
20   IF A<B THEN 80
30   IF A>B THEN 60
40   PRINT "EQUAL NUMBERS";A
50   GOTO 90
60   PRINT B,A
70   GOTO 90
80   PRINT A,B
90   END


RUN
ORDER    1049

?23,67
  23             67

DONE AT 1049
RUN
ORDER    1049

?76,12
  12             76

DONE AT 1049
```

An alternative to the GOTO statements in lines 50 and 70 would be to use a STOP statement. STOP is equivalent to GOTO followed by the line number of the END statement. For example:

20 STOP

is equivalent to

20 GOTO 80
. . .
. . .
80 END

Flowchart for
program ORDER

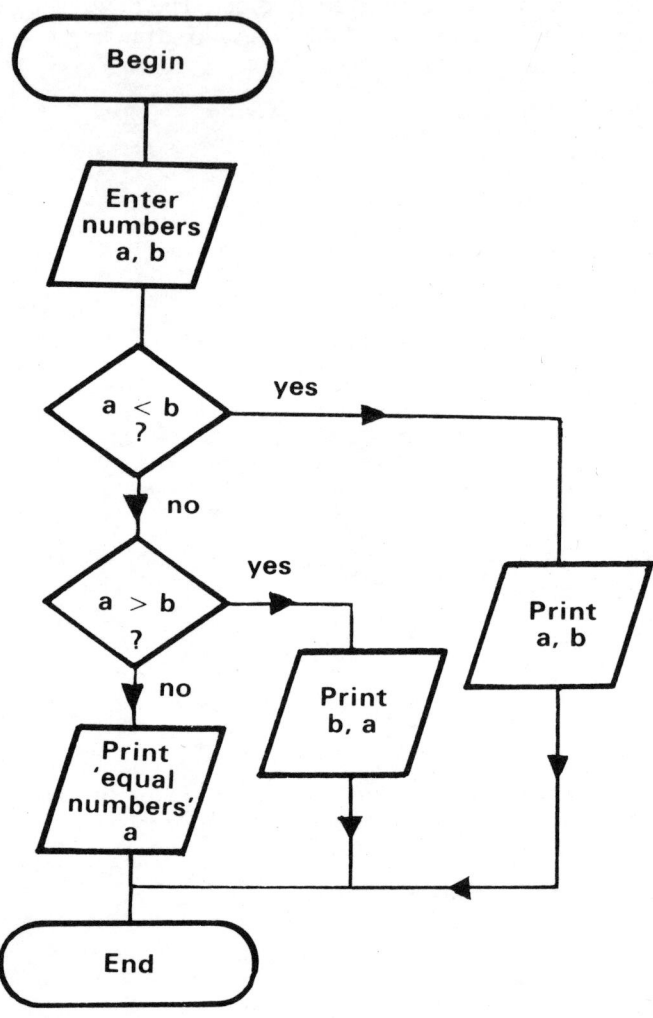

This is only the beginning of sorting. Problem 2B.3 goes a little further and various methods are discussed in Chapter 6.

Problems 2B

2B.1   How many even numbers have to be added together, starting with 2, then 4, then 6 etc., for the sum to exceed 100, 200, ...? Can you adapt your program to find the sum of the first 10, 20, 50, ... even numbers?

2B.2   For a positive whole number, N, N factorial (written $N!$) means the result of multiplying all the whole numbers from 1 up to N. So $4!$ means $1 \times 2 \times 3 \times 4$ $(=24)$ and $6!$ means $1 \times 2 \times 3 \times 4 \times 5 \times 6$ $(=720)$. Write a program to calculate $N!$ for any input N.

2B.3   Write a program to take three numbers as input and print them out in ascending order of magnitude. Assume to begin with that the numbers cannot be equal. Can you adapt your program to deal with the cases when two or three of the numbers might be equal? Can you extend your method to deal with four numbers, five numbers . . .?

2B.4   The chance that at least two people in a group of n share the same birthday is given by

$$1 - \frac{365 \times 364 \times 363 \times 362 \times \ldots \times (366 - n)}{365^n}.$$

Calculate the chances for groups of 2, 3, 4, ... people. How many people must there be in the group for the chance that two of them share the same birthday to be better than $\frac{1}{2}$?

2B.5   By calculating the values of $y = 24 - x - x^2$ as x increases in steps of 1 from -5, find (to the nearest whole number) the maximum value of $24 - x - x^2$. Can you find the maximum value to a greater accuracy?

2B.6   Write a program that will accept, as input, the ages of the pupils in a school and calculate the numbers in the age ranges – under 13, 13 or over but under 16, 16 or over but under 17, over 17. Can you adjust your program to give the required information as percentages of the school population?

Special functions

Many mathematical calculations involve expressions which cannot easily be stated in terms of $+$, $-$, $*$, $/$ and $\uparrow$. A particular example would be an expression involving a square root. In BASIC, the difficulty is avoided by the availability of special functions which enable the programmer to call up expressions, such as square root, in a single statement. The form of the square root function is SQR(X). X can be any expression providing its value is not negative. As with expressions in assignment statements, this expression will be evaluated according to the normal rules of algebra. The following are all valid statements:

20 LET $A = SQR(X)$

20 LET $A = SQR(3\cdot14)$

20 LET $A = SQR(A + 3\cdot5 * B)$

20 LET $A = B - SQR(A * B - 4)$.

It is even permissible to include a square root function within a square root function:

20 LET $A = SQR(2 * B + SQR(1 + A))$.

The functions available will depend on the system being used, but some of the common ones are:

SQR(X) gives the square root of the expression X. X must have a non-negative value.

ABS(X) gives the absolute value of the expression X, that is the numeric value disregarding sign. Thus ABS($-2\cdot1$) has the value $2\cdot1$.

INT(X) gives the integer (whole number) part of the expression X, i.e. the largest integer which is not larger than X. For example:

if $X = $ $3\cdot4$,   INT(X) has the value 3
if $X = $ $-3\cdot4$,   INT(X) has the value -4.

The following more advanced mathematical functions are amongst those available on most BASIC systems.

$SIN(X)$ gives the sine of the expression (X). X is in radians

$COS(X)$ gives the cosine of the expression (X). X is in radians

$TAN(X)$ gives the tangent of the expression (X). X is in radians. If the TAN function is not available it can of course be calculated from the SIN and COS functions

$ATN(X)$ gives the angle (in radians) whose tangent is the expression (X).

$LOG(X)$ gives the natural logarithm of the expression (X) – i.e. the logarithm to the base 'e'. X must have a positive value

$EXP(X)$ gives the value of the constant 'e' raised to a power equal to the value of the expression (X).

These are common to virtually all versions of BASIC. Other functions will be explained as there is a need for them.

An example of the use of one of these functions is shown in the program DIVID which follows. This program tests if one whole number is exactly divisible by another and uses the fact that, for a whole number, both the number and INT (the number) have the same value. The program simply carries out the division and tests to see if the result is a whole number.

We could make the program even shorter by replacing statements 20 and 30 by the single statement.

20 IF $INT(A/B) = A/B$ THEN 60

in other words, an IF statement is not restricted to relations between variables but may also contain relations between two expressions, or between a variable and an expression, e.g.

20 IF $A = B + C/2$ THEN 100
30 IF $A + B + C > X + Y$ THEN 70.

```
LIST
DIVID

10    INPUT A,B
20    LET D=A/B
30    IF INT(D)=D THEN 60
40    PRINT A;"IS NOT EXACTLY DIVISIBLE BY ";B
50    STOP
60    PRINT A;"IS EXACTLY DIVISIBLE BY ";B
70    END


RUN
DIVID    1056

?144,12
 144   IS EXACTLY DIVISIBLE BY   12

DONE AT 1057
RUN
DIVID    1057

?145,12
 145   IS NOT EXACTLY DIVISIBLE BY   12

DONE AT 1057
```

Problems 2C

2C.1 Write a program to test whether a given number is even or odd, in a different way from that used for 1C.6.

2C.2 Prepare a table of sines, cosines and tangents for angles from 0° to 90° in steps of 10°.

2C.3 Write a program to update a team's record in a football league table (games played, wins, losses, draws, goals for, goals against, points). The input data should be as simple as possible.

2C.4 In problem 1C.5 three numbers were tested to see if they could form the sides of a right-angled triangle. Now write a program to test three numbers to see if they can form the sides of any triangle, or if they form no triangle at all. Can you also test if the triangle is obtuse angled?

2C.5 A factor of a number is any number which will divide exactly into the given number. For example, 2 and 3 are factors of 6 (and so is 6, as every number divides exactly into itself). Write a program to find the largest factor, other than itself, of a given number. Can you extend this to find all the factors of the number?

2C.6 A 'perfect' number is one whose factors, apart from itself, add up to the number. Write a program to find perfect numbers.

Note: this program will take a lot of computer time if more than 2 perfect numbers are found.

2C.7 In the quadratic equation $3x^2 + 2x - 6 = 0$, the numbers $+3$, $+2$, and -6 are called the coefficients of the equation. Write a program to input the coefficients of a quadratic equation and calculate the solutions of the equation. Does your program allow for two solutions being the same? Does it allow for there being only one solution?

2C.8 Input a list of numbers and print out the largest together with its position in the input list.

Summary of the main points of Chapter Two

The order of evaluating expressions is:

  i) calculations within brackets
  ii) ↑ – raising to a power
  iii) * and /
  iv) + and − .

Other than this, an expression is evaluated from left to right.

IF statements can involve the following conditions:

$$=, <, >, <=, >=, <>.$$

Standard functions are available, these include:

SQR(X)	ABS(X)	INT(X)
SIN(X)	COS(X)	TAN(X)
ATN(X)	LOG(X)	EXP(X)

The SIN, COS and TAN functions all require X to be in radians. LOG(X) finds the natural logarithm of the expression X.

Chapter 3

Character Handling

Output of text

In the previous chapters, a PRINT statement has been used to produce headings and so give clarity to the results. The program PRINTS, which follows, illustrates this and introduces several new printing features.

```
PRINTS     16:10    G265 B 01/08/72

10    LET A=5.6
20    LET B=6.725
30    LET C=7
40    PRINT A,B,C
50    PRINT
60    PRINT A;B;C
70    PRINT
80    PRINT A;B;C;
90    PRINT A*B;A
100   PRINT
110   PRINT "TOM   DICK   HARRY   ";
120   PRINT " JOHN   FRED"
130   PRINT
140   PRINT " A EQUALS ";A
150   PRINT "A TIMES B EQUALS ";A*B
160   PRINT
170   PRINT "'A' EQUALS ";A;" B = ";B;" 'C' IS ";C
180   END

RUN


PRINTS     16:11    G265 B 01/08/72

 5.6              6.725           7

 5.6     6.725    7

 5.6     6.725    7   37.66    5.6

TOM    DICK   HARRY   JOHN    FRED

 A EQUALS  5.6
A TIMES B EQUALS   37.66

'A' EQUALS  5.6    B =   6.725    'C' IS   7
```

Particular features which should be noted are as follows:

Statement 50   Empty PRINT statement produces on extra line feed.

Statement 60   The ; instead of , compresses printing. The degree of compression will depend on the system used.

Statement 80   The terminating ; suppresses line-feed.

Statement 90   The suppressed line-feed of statement 80 causes the printing under statement 90 to continue on the same line. This statement also illustrates the facility of including an expression in a PRINT statement. The expression is evaluated and then printed, thus saving a line of program.

Statement 140 A combination of text and values. In this case the semi-colon causes the value of A to be printed immediately following "A EQUALS".

Statement 150 Note the importance of spaces within quotes.

An INPUT statement sends a '?' to the teleprinter inviting the user to respond with the appropriate input value. Using this in conjunction with the facility to suppress line-feed, by means of a semi-colon at the end of a PRINT statement, enables a question to be sent to the user of the teleprinter. The programs QUEST1 and QUEST2 show this.

```
READY.

LIST

QUEST1     15:33     G265 H 01/08/72

10 PRINT "WHAT IS THE VALUE OF 'A'";
20 INPUT A
30 PRINT "THE VALUE OF 'A' IS ";A
40 END

RUN



QUEST1     15:33     G265 H 01/08/72

WHAT IS THE VALUE OF 'A'? 67.98
THE VALUE OF 'A' IS   67.98
```

```
LIST

QUEST2      15:35     G265 B 01/08/72

10 PRINT "A = ";
20 INPUT A
30 PRINT "'A' HAS THE VALUE ";A
40 END

RUN



QUEST2      15:35     G265 B 01/08/72

A = ? 23.543
'A' HAS THE VALUE  23.543
```

Output of text is frequently used to clarify the printout. Good documentation is essential if the printout is to be read by some person other than the programmer. Indeed, good documentation is an aid to the programmer himself.

The principle of good documentation also extends to the program, for it is difficult to follow through and check a long and involved program. A facility which exists to aid this documentation is the REM statement which enables the programmer to add notes to explain what is happening at various stages in the program. For example:

```
10 REM     THIS IS A SIMPLE PROGRAM
20 REM     FIRST INPUT THE DATA
30 INPUT A,B,C
40 LET D=C+B
50 LET E=D*A
60 REM ****CALCULATIONS COMPLETE****
70 PRINT A;B;C;D;E
80 END
```

The REM statements are completely ignored at run time and so do not add to the execution time as would a series of PRINT statements. Typical remarks may be to identify the programmer or the project if these are not indicated in the program name. Since the text written after REM is ignored, some programmers prefer to write the full word REMARK.

Strings and string variables

We have seen that BASIC can easily process variables which are related by some algebraic expression. A most important feature of computer languages is that many of them allow us to process non-numeric information, such as words.

A series of characters is known as a 'string'. The set of characters usually contains all the letters of the alphabet, the digits and a number of symbols e.g. * / £ & : ? @ + space . A string in BASIC is any series of these characters and can be uniquely defined by enclosing the characters in quotes. For example:

"ABCDEFG"
"A BASIC PROGRAM"
"JOHN SMITH, 10 HIGH STREET, LONDON, W11."

It is usual for there to be a limit to the number of characters in a string; we shall restrict ourselves to 40 characters.

It is convenient to be able to refer to a string by name. This name is a variable, similar to a numeric variable, and is referred to as a string variable. String variable names are the same as numeric variable names but with the addition of a distinguishing $ or £ symbol: e.g. $A\$$, $B\$$, $X\$$. So we have an extension to our original set of statements:

INPUT $A\$$

PRINT $A\$$

IF $A\$ = B\$$ THEN 20

LET $A\$ = $ "A STRING"

LET $X\$ = A\$$

IF $A\$ = $ "YES" THEN 20

IF $A\$ < > B\$$ THEN 20

Some BASIC systems require us to reserve space in the memory to store each string variable. This is done by a DIMension statement, which can be placed at any part of the program, giving the maximum length of each string; e.g. DIM $A\$(10)$, $B\$(20)$. This is not the usual use of the DIM statement and, except where indicated, programs in this book have not been run on systems requiring it.

Example

Draw a flowchart and then write a program which counts the number of times a word occurs in a sentence.

**Flowchart for
program COUNT1**

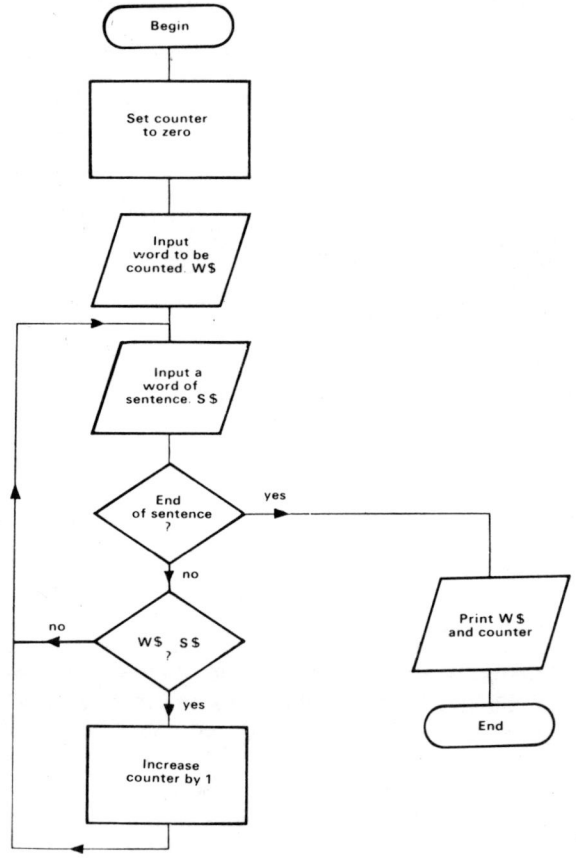

LIST

```
COUNT1     15:40     G265 B 01/08/72

10 LET C=0
20 INPUT WS
25 PRINT
30 INPUT SS
40 IF SS="." THEN 85
50 IF SS=WS THEN 70
60 GOTO 30
70 LET C=C+1
80 GOTO 30
85 PRINT
90 PRINT "THE WORD '";WS;"' OCCURS ";C;" TIMES"
100 END

RUN



COUNT1     15:41     G265 B 01/08/72

? THE

? THE
? CAT
? SAT
? ON
? THE
? OTHER
? CAT
? .

THE WORD 'THE' OCCURS  2  TIMES
```

Example

A group of six workmen are engaged on a building site in the country. Each week two of them are responsible for brewing the tea and they take the job in turn, only one man being changed each week. Draw a flowchart and then write a program to print pairs of names for this job for a period of six weeks.

**Flowchart for
program TROTA**

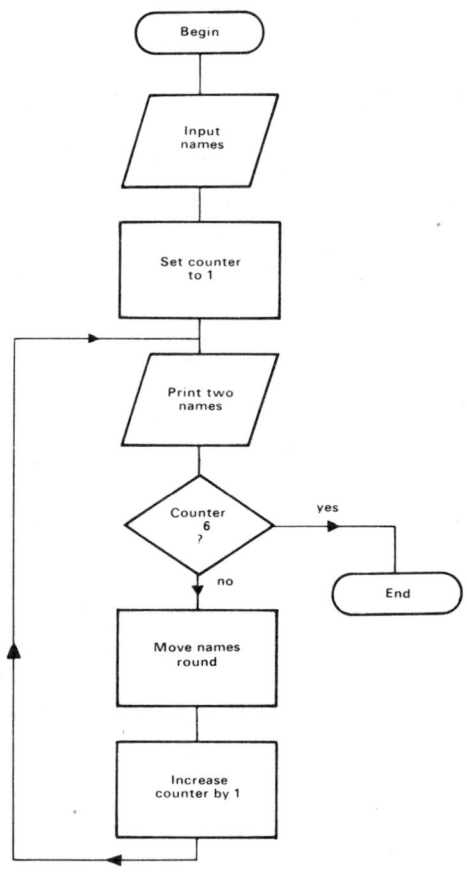

```
LIST


TRUTA        15:58    G265 B 01/08/72

10  INPUT AΣ,BΣ,CΣ,DΣ,EΣ,FΣ
20  LET C=1
30  PRINT AΣ;"  AND  ";BΣ;"  FOR WEEK  ";C
40  IF C=6 THEN 140
50  LET XΣ=AΣ
60  LET AΣ=BΣ
70  LET BΣ=CΣ
80  LET CΣ=DΣ
90  LET DΣ=EΣ
100 LET EΣ=FΣ
110 LET FΣ=XΣ
120 LET C=C+1
130 GOTO 30
140 END

RUN


TRUTA        15:59    G265 B 01/08/72

? SMITH,BROWN,JONES,JAMES,DAVIS,SNAPE
SMITH   AND   BROWN   FOR WEEK   1
BROWN   AND   JONES   FOR WEEK   2
JONES   AND   JAMES   FOR WEEK   3
JAMES   AND   DAVIS   FOR WEEK   4
DAVIS   AND   SNAPE   FOR WEEK   5
SNAPE   AND   SMITH   FOR WEEK   6
```

It is possible to produce programs in BASIC which can be used by a person with little or no knowledge of programming or of using a terminal. These programs involve self-explanatory text produced by PRINT statements. The development of programs for Computer Aided Instruction always makes use of this facility.

Even what appears to be quite a simple program becomes very complex as it is necessary to make provision for unexpected responses from the user. This is shown in statement 110 of the program TALK which follows where provision is made for the question (statement 70) to be asked repeatedly if neither 'YES' nor 'NO' is given in reply.

Note: On the system used to run the program TALK, a '#' is printed for a '%'.

```
LIST

TALK        16:15    G265 B 01/08/72

20  PRINT "WHAT IS YOUR NAME,PLEASE";
30  INPUT A£
40  PRINT "HELLO ";A£;". HOW MANY MARKS DID YOU GET IN ";
50  PRINT "YOUR LAST TEST ";
60  INPUT M
70  PRINT "WAS THAT MARK A PERCENTAGE ";
80  INPUT B£
90  IF B£="YES" THEN 140
100 IF B£="NO" THEN 250
110 PRINT "PLEASE ANSWER WITH 'YES' OR 'NO' "
120 GOTO 70
140 IF M>90 THEN 200
150 IF M>70 THEN 210
160 IF M>40 THEN 220
170 PRINT M;"# IS'NT REALLY VERY GOOD ";A£;" IS IT?"
180 PRINT " YOU MUST DO BETTER NEXT TIME"
190 STOP
200 PRINT M;"# IS VERY GOOD ";A£;" VERY WELL DONE"
205 STOP
210 PRINT M;"# IS GOOD ";A£;" ,WELL DONE"
215 STOP
220 PRINT M;"# IS QUITE GOOD ";A£;" KEEP WORKING HARD"
225 STOP
250 PRINT "PLEASE CONVERT YOUR MARK TO A # "
260 PRINT "WHAT # DID YOU GET ";A£;" ";
270 INPUT M
280 GOTO 140
290 END

RUN



TALK        16:17    G265 B 01/08/72

WHAT IS YOUR NAME,PLEASE? FRED
HELLO FRED. HOW MANY MARKS DID YOU GET IN YOUR LAST TEST ? 35
WAS THAT MARK A PERCENTAGE ? NO
PLEASE CONVERT YOUR MARK TO A #
WHAT # DID YOU GET FRED ? 40
  40    # IS'NT REALLY VERY GOOD FRED IS IT?
    YOU MUST DO BETTER NEXT TIME
```

Problems 3A

3A.1 Write a program which prints out the words UN, DEUX, TROIS, QUATRE, CINQ in that order all on one line; then in that order on separate lines and finally in reverse order on one line.

3A.2 Write a program for young children to use which tests their arithmetic ability. A print-out could look like this:

> PLEASE TYPE THE ANSWER TO EACH PROBLEM AFTER THE '?'
> $16+25 = $? 31
> WRONG JOHN. PLEASE TRY AGAIN
> $16+25 = $? 41
> GOOD. NOW THE NEXT
> $52+17 = $? 69
> WELL DONE   etc.

3A.3 Append counters to your program for problem 3A.2 which counts the number of times the pupils get the problem right first time, second time, wrong, etc.

3A.4 Write a program which prints out the day of the week for a particular date, given one day and date in the same month.

3A.5 Amend your solution to problem 1C.4 so that it is self-explanatory to the user.

3A.6 Modify your solution to problem 2C.3 so that the user is requested to input data at the appropriate time.

An alternative input statement

It is possible to input data into a program in BASIC with statements other than INPUT. This requires you to add a DATA statement to the program, which contains the items of data separated by commas.

　　e.g. DATA 10, 20, 25, 12, 16

Data is input from a DATA statement by means of a READ statement. Character string and numeric data may appear in the same DATA statement. Thus corresponding to:

　　20 READ *A*, *B*, *X*$, *N*

could be the DATA statement

　　120 DATA 29·3, 7, "MR SMITH", 29

This form of input of data is obligatory when running a batch of BASIC programs without need for intervention by the computer operator. This method of running computer programs is commonly termed 'batch processing'.

To show the use of these statements, let us simply input a list of numbers and then print them out together with the sum of adjacent pairs. This is shown in the program SUMS.

```
LIST

SUMS          16:34     G265 B 01/08/72

10  READ A,B,C,D,E
20  PRINT A;B;C;D;E
30  PRINT A+B;B+C;C+D;D+E;E+A
40  DATA 10,20,25,12,16
50  END

RUN


SUMS          16:35     G265 B 01/08/72

10      20      25      12      16
30      45      37      28      26
```

The position of the DATA statement in the program is not important and there may be more than one. The READ will start at the beginning of the list in the first DATA statement and continue from statement to statement automatically as necessary. A 'pointer' keeps check on which data item is to be read next and so two READ statements in different parts of a program can take alternate data items from the list. This is shown in a program which calculates simple interest on various amounts of capital over 4 different periods of time, for each amount, at a fixed interest rate. The program, SIMINT, and its associated flowchart follow.

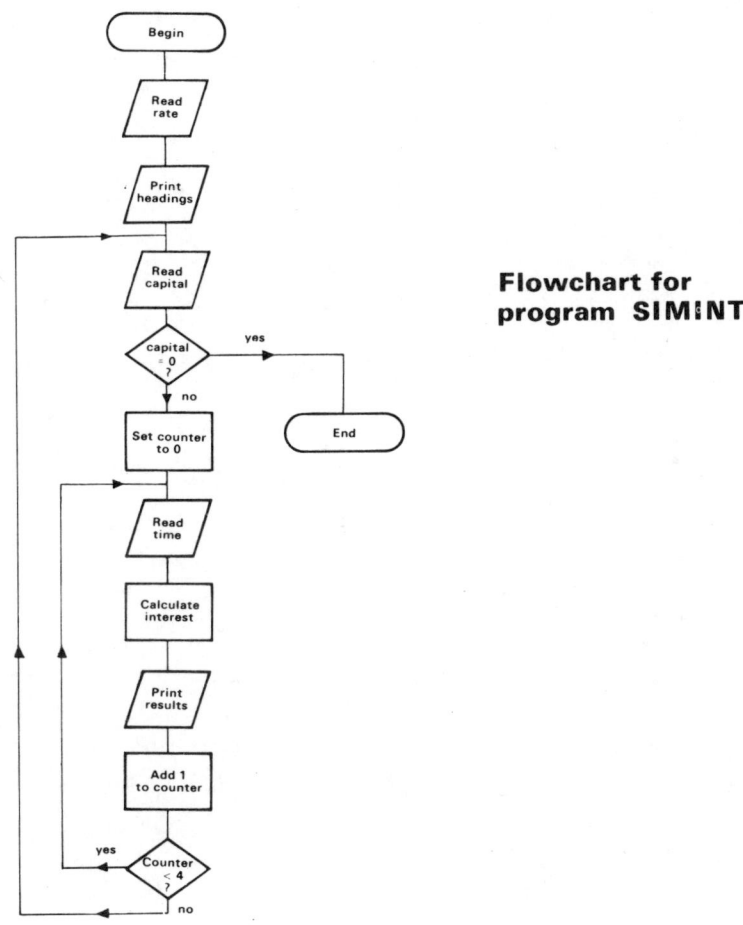

Flowchart for program SIMINT

Clearly it is necessary to arrange the data in a precise order otherwise the numbers would be assigned to the wrong variable names. The way in which the data is arranged is known as the 'data structure'. For this job, we use a data structure as follows:

> rate, 1st capital, time, time, time, time, 2nd capital, time, time, time, time, 3rd capital, time, time, _____, 'dummy' capital

The end of the data list is indicated by a dummy item, in this case, zero, which is used to terminate the program execution.

```
LIST

SIMINT     16:06     G265  B  01/08/72

10  READ R
20  PRINT "CAPITAL          TIME            RATE           AMOUNT"
25  READ C
30  IF C=0 THEN 130
40  LET I=0
50  READ T
60  LET A=(C*T*R)/100
70  PRINT C,T,R,A
80  LET I=I+1
90  IF I<4 THEN 50
100 GOTO 25
110 DATA 7.5,500,3,5,7,9,785,1,2,3,4
120 DATA 450,10,15,20,25,0
130 END

RUN


SIMINT     16:06     G265  B  01/08/72
```

CAPITAL	TIME	RATE	AMOUNT
500	3	7.5	112.5
500	5	7.5	187.5
500	7	7.5	262.5
500	9	7.5	337.5
785	1	7.5	58.875
785	2	7.5	117.75
785	3	7.5	176.625
785	4	7.5	235.5
450	10	7.5	337.5
450	15	7.5	506.25
450	20	7.5	675
450	25	7.5	843.75

The structure of the data for a certain job will depend on a number of factors including:

   a) The way in which the data is collected
   b) The most efficient way for the computer to handle the data
   c) The actual input devices being used by that computer system.

After considering these factors the data can be arranged and the program written.

In the following problems, the data structure is given and programs should be written to perform the required task on that data structure.

Problems 3B

3B.1   A file held in DATA statements has the following structure:

SURNAME, CHRISTIAN NAME, ADDRESS.

Write a program which asks for a surname and then prints out the full name and address. The format should be suitable for addressing an envelope.

3B.2   Rewrite your program for problem 1A.5 with the data held in DATA statements.

3B.3   Decide upon a suitable structure for the data of problem 1C.4 and rewrite your program using this.

3B.4   Find the average height of a number of groups of people. The number in each group is not the same. The data is organised in the following way;

number in the group

list of heights

number in the next group

list of heights

number in the next group

list of heights .... and so on.

If you are interested in statistics you could extend this program to test if there was any significant height variation between the groups.

3B.5 At the end of the season it is interesting to calculate the average runs
scored by all the batsmen in a cricket club. The data structure could be:

Batsman's Name

Total runs

No. of innings

No. of times 'not out'

Batsman's name

Total runs

No. of innings

No. of times 'not out' .... and so on.

Write a program to read data of this sort and then calculate the average.
The output could be tabulated as follows:

NAME   TOTAL RUNS   NO. OF INNINGS   AVERAGE

We can later arrange to sort these results into order of performance.

3B.6 A number of DATA statements contain a list of names of pupils in a
class. The marks scored by the pupils are to be entered through the
teleprinter under an INPUT statement and the program should produce
a tabulated list of names and scores.

Data files

It is possible to read items from a DATA statement more than once, resetting the pointer to the beginning of the list of items, by the use of the RESTORE statement. The program REVERS, which shows the use of the RESTORE statement, has a list of six names in a DATA statement and prints these out in reverse order.

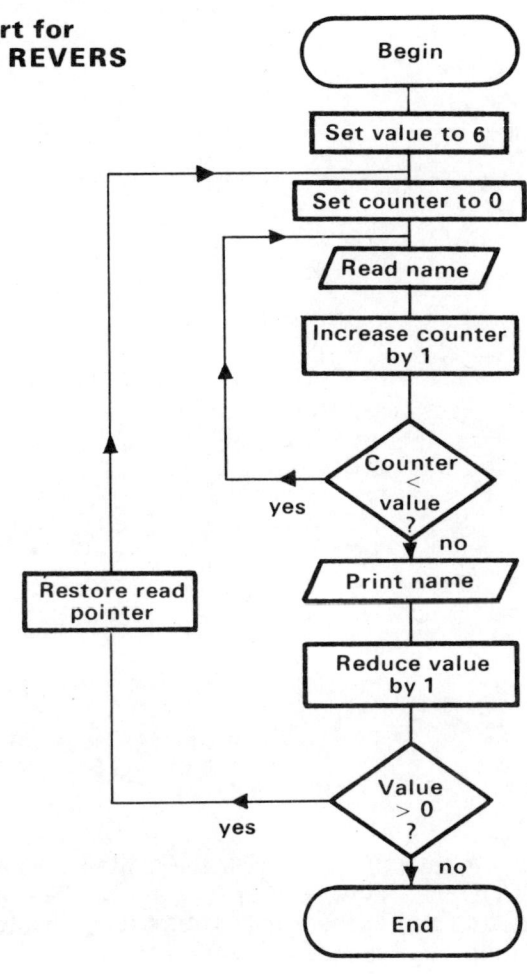

Flowchart for program REVERS

In a program like REVERS the DATA statement is used as a place to store information. In data processing terms, such a store of information is referred to as a **file**. This type of file is called a sequential access file because the items can only be accessed in order. This means that it may take some time to access an item well down the list. In chapter 7 random access files are introduced which allow large amounts of data to be investigated quickly.

```
LIST

REVERS     10:27    G265 B 01/08/72

20    LET N=6
30    LET C=0
40    READ A$
50    LET C=C+1
60    IF C<N THEN 40
70    PRINT A$
80    LET N=N-1
85    RESTORE
90    IF N>0 THEN 30
95    DATA "HARRY","JOHN","FRED","ALBERT","GEORGE","WILLIAM"
100   END

RUN


REVERS     10:27    G265 B 01/08/72

WILLIAM
GEORGE
ALBERT
FRED
JOHN
HARRY
```

The DATA statement can be used as a file in the analysis of some text in a rather neater way than COUNT1, shown earlier. The text can be stored in a series of DATA statements and then interrogated. Use of this is made in the program COUNT2 in the following example.

Example

Write a program which asks for a series of words to be input at the teleprinter and counts the occurrences of each in text stored in DATA statements. The solution given is based on the previous program, COUNT1.

```
     LIST

     COUNT2    15:51   G265 B 01/08/72

     20 PRINT "TYPE THE WORD TO BE COUNTED AFTER '?'"
     30 PRINT "WHEN YOU HAVE FINISHED TYPE 'ZZZ'"
     40 LET C=0
     50 RESTORE
     60 INPUT W£
     70 IF W£="ZZZ" THEN 250
     80 READ S£
     90 IF S£="ZZZ" THEN 140
     100 IF S£=W£ THEN 120
     110 GOTO 80
     120 LET C=C+1
     130 GOTO 80
     140 PRINT "'";W£;"' OCCURS ";C;" TIMES"
     150 GOTO 40
     160 DATA THE,MOLE,FLUNG,BACK,HIS,SCULLS,WITH,A,FLOURISH,",","
     170 DATA AND,MADE,A,GREAT,DIG,AT,THE,WATER,".",HE,MISSED
     180 DATA THE,SURFACE,ALTOGETHER,",",HIS,LEGS,FLEW,UP,ABOVE
     190 DATA HIS,HEAD,",",AND,HE,FOUND,HIMSELF,LYING,ON,THE
     200 DATA TOP,OF,THE,RAT,".",GREATLY,ALARMED,",",HE,MADE
     210 DATA A,GRAB,AT,THE,SIDE,OF,THE,BOAT,",",AND,THE,NEXT
     220 DATA MOMENT,"--",SPLOOSH,".","
     230 DATA ZZZ
     250 END
     RUN


     COUNT2    15:53    G265 B 01/08/72

     TYPE THE WORD TO BE COUNTED AFTER '?'
     WHEN YOU HAVE FINISHED TYPE 'ZZZ'
     ? AT
     'AT' OCCURS   2   TIMES
     ? HE
     'HE' OCCURS   3   TIMES
     ? THE
     'THE' OCCURS   8   TIMES
     ? BADGER
     'BADGER' OCCURS   0   TIMES
     ? .
     '.' OCCURS   3   TIMES
     ? ZZZ
```

Stock records

In commercial computing, one major job is the control of stock in a shop or warehouse. A series of DATA statements may be used to provide a file of items in stock. The data structure for each item could be:

Item name	number in stock	minimum stock level	cost of item

A stock file could be made up of a number of such records. This file may need to be interrogated in a number of ways.

1. To find out the number in stock of a particular item.

2. To find out which items are below the minimum stock level, so that re-ordering can be done.

3. To find the value of the present stock.

4. To print out the full stock file.

5. To cost an order from a customer of a number of purchases of various items.

As an example of the use of this type of file, the program STKCHK allows the first of these investigations to be made. A problem with this method is that it is not possible to change any of the records easily, for example as items are issued from stock. This type of 'read-only' file is of value only when the records do not often change. The procedure of changing the contents of a file is known as 'up-dating' the file. Files which can be changed will be used in chapter 7.

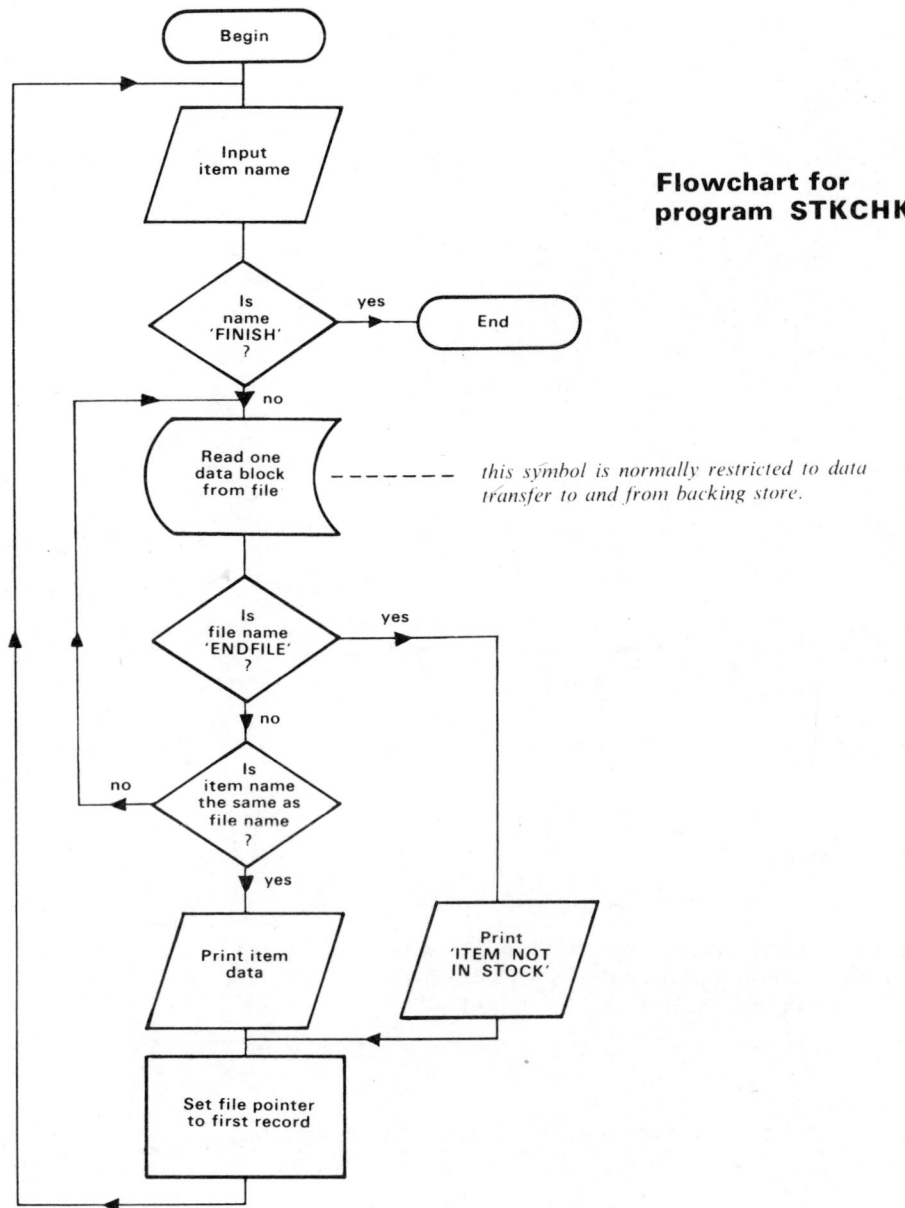

Flowchart for program STKCHK

this symbol is normally restricted to data transfer to and from backing store.

```
LIST


STKCHK      15:27      G265 B 01/08/72

10  INPUT I£
20  IF I£="FINISH" THEN 180
30  READ R£,R1,R2,R3
40  IF R£="ENDFILE" THEN 150
50  IF I£ <> R£ THEN 30
60  PRINT "ITEM ";R£;" STOCK IS ";R1
70  RESTORE
80  GOTO 10
90  DATA NUTS,5000,2500,1
100 DATA WASHERS,250,200,2
110 DATA NAILS,4000,4500,.5
120 DATA HAMMERS,50,45,100
130 DATA RIVETS,5000,3000,1
140 DATA ENDFILE,0,0,0
150 PRINT "ITEM NOT IN STOCK"
160 RESTORE
170 GOTO 10
180 END


RUN
WAIT.


STKCHK      15:28      G265 B 01/08/72

? NAILS
ITEM NAILS STOCK IS   4000
? NUTS
ITEM NUTS STOCK IS   5000
? BOLTS
ITEM NOT IN STOCK
? RIVETS
ITEM RIVETS STOCK IS   5000
? FINISH
```

Note:
In addition to using single letters $A, B, C, \ldots$ as variables, BASIC allows the use of a letter followed by a single digit. For example: $N1, N2, N3, \ldots$: In statement 30, this form of a variable has been used.

Problems 3C

3C.1 Write a program to allow a second interrogation of the data file in STKCHK (statements 90–140) printing a list of those items for which the stock is below the 'minimum stock level'.

3C.2 Write a program to produce a tabulated printout of all the items in stock.

3C.3 The text analysis program, COUNT2, counts the words in the text. Write a program to count the total number of sentences and the number of words in each sentence.

3C.4 Is the text written in the first person? In which tense are the main clauses? There are many other investigations which can be made.

3C.5 It is possible, though not very easy, to sort a set of numbers into order by storing them in a DATA statement and then searching along for the smallest and then printing it out. Then search for the next smallest and so on. Other sorting methods can be used after we have looked at subscripted variables in the next chapter.

3C.6 In BASIC each character is given a numeric code and these are compared. In this way it is possible to compare two characters and say that one is 'larger' than the other. It is also possible to say that one string is 'larger' than another. Write a program which allows you to discover the way this coding works and hence, sort a few words into alphabetical order.

Summary of the main points of Chapter Three

Remember the effect of PRINT
             PRINT A, B
             PRINT A;

A REM statement may be used for adding notes to a program.

A string is a group of characters, normally enclosed in quotes.

The use of the string constants and string variables is similar to that of numeric constants and variables.

   e.g. INPUT $A\$$
        PRINT $A\$$
        IF $A\$ = B\$$ THEN 20
        IF $A\$ = $ "YES" THEN 20
        IF $A\$ < > B\$$ THEN 20
        LET $A\$ = $ "A STRING"
        LET $A\$ = X\$$

In some systems a DIM statement must be included in a program to define the maximum length of each string variable.

READ is an alternative to INPUT for numeric and string data. The data may be read from one or more DATA statements. Numeric and non-numeric data may be included in the same DATA statement, a character string being enclosed in quotes on most systems.

Chapter 4

Loops and Arrays

Control of loops

You may have tackled problem 1C.3 earlier in your work. The problem was to 'produce a table of squares and cubes of the integers from 1 to 10 inclusive'.

The solution to this problem must have included:

 i) A counter, originally set to zero
 ii) An instruction to increase the counter by 1
iii) A test to see if the counter had reached 10, and the necessary branch.

For example:

```
20 LET C=0
30 LET C=C+1
40
50
60
70
80 IF C<10 THEN 30
90 END
```

This program allows the execution of statements 40, 50, 60, 70 just 10 times.

BASIC allows us to perform loops like this one in a simpler way. It also makes it easier to see that we have not gone round the loop once too often or once too few which is a common error.

The new statements are a pair which must always be used together. They are FOR and NEXT and act like brackets to the section of program between them.

The example now simplifies to:

```
20 FOR C=1 TO 10
40
50
60
70
80 NEXT C
90 END
```

71

The statements 40 ... 70 are executed 10 times. On the first execution $C = 1$, the second $C = 2, \ldots$, the tenth execution $C = 10$. Thus the effect is exactly the same as for the previous statements 20, 30, ..., 80.

A revised program (POWERS), using a FOR statement, for the table of squares and cubes follows.

Program 'POWERS'

```
LIST
0010 PRINT " X                X↑2            X↑3"
0020 FOR X=1 TO 10
0030    PRINT X,X↑2,X↑3
0040 NEXT X
0050 END


RUN
 X                      X↑2              X↑3
  1                      1                1
  2                      4                8
  3                      9               27
  4                     16               64
  5                     25              125
  6                     36              216
  7                     49              343
  8                     64              512
  9                     81              729
 10                    100             1000

*READY
```

Note: Most of the programs in this chapter have been run on a small time-sharing system which, at present, has no disc storage. There is consequently no name allocated to a program since it cannot be saved. Names given in the text are merely for reference.

Problems 4A

4A.1 Problem 1A.5 calculates the charge for a taxi journey. Print out a table of charges for distances of 1 mile to 10 miles in intervals of 1 mile, using the data given.

4A.2 In problem 2B.2, $N!$ was defined as $1 \times 2 \times 3 \times 4 \times 5 \times 6 \times \ldots \times N$, where N is a whole number. Rewrite the solution to this problem, using a FOR loop.

4A.3 The Fibonacci sequence starts with the numbers 1 and 1. The next number is the sum of these and subsequent numbers are the sum of the preceeding pair. So we get:

1, 1, 2, 3, 5, 8, 13, 21, ...

Write a program which prints the first 30 Fibonacci numbers. Print also the ratio of adjacent numbers.

4A.4 Write a program which tabulates values of $SIN(X)$ for values of X between 0 and 20 degrees. Remember to convert from degrees to radians before using the sine function.

4A.5 It is possible to calculate $\sin x$ by summing the series

$$\frac{x}{1!} - \frac{x^3}{3!} + \frac{x^5}{5!} - \frac{x^7}{7!} + \ldots .$$

Calculate $\sin x$ by this summation using 6 terms under the control of a FOR loop for values of x between 0 and 20 degrees.

4A.6 Calculate values of y where $y = 2x^3 - 7x^2 + 10x - 17$ for $x = -5$ to $+5$ in steps of 1.

Varying the step size

So far we have used only positive unit steps in our loop. The step size can be varied in any desired way as shown in the examples below:

```
FOR N = 1 TO 10 STEP 2
FOR N = 0 TO 100 STEP 10
FOR N = 100 TO 50 STEP -2
FOR N = A TO B STEP (B-A)/10 .
```

Without the use of STEP the step length is assumed to be 1. In the last example care must be taken to ensure that the FOR statement will work for all expected values of the variables. The way to discover the exact way in which the statements work is to write simple programs and run them. For example:

```
10 INPUT A,B
20 FOR N=A TO B STEP (B-A)/10
30 PRINT N
40 NEXT N
50 END
```

What happens if $B < A$?

How does the computer handle FOR $N = 10$ TO 20 STEP 3?

Try these and others. Don't forget that depression of the BREAK key allows you to escape from a loop which repeats itself more often than you expect!

It is often valuable to 'nest' FOR loops when tabulating values of expressions containing a number of variables. For example, suppose we wished to calculate the value of $A^2/(A^2 + B^2)$ for a series of values of A and B. We would set A to its first value and then let B vary over its whole range. Then A could take its second value and so on. This is shown in the program NESTS.

Program 'NESTS'

```
LIST
0010 FOR A=1 TO 4
0020    FOR B=1 TO 2
0030       PRINT A;B;A↑2/(A↑2+B↑2)
0040    NEXT B
0050 NEXT A
0060 END

RUN
 1   1   .5
 1   2   .2
 2   1   .8
 2   2   .5
 3   1   .9
 3   2   .692308
 4   1   .941176
 4   2   .8

*READY
```

A more ambitious use of nested loops is shown in the following example.

If three dice are being rolled, it is of interest to know what the chance is of a particular total occurring. This can be calculated using probability theory but it may also be found by trial and error. The program DICE shows how this is done.

Flowchart for program DICE

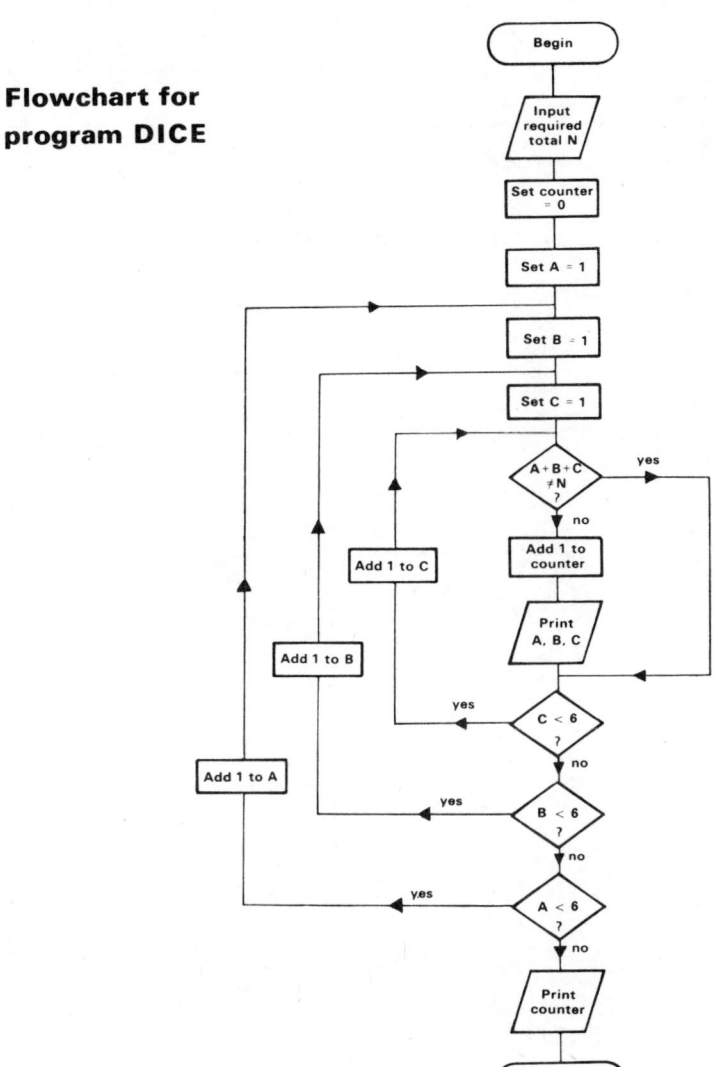

Program 'DICE'

```
LIST
0010 INPUT N
0015 PRINT
0020 LET K=0
0030 FOR A=1 TO 6
0040    FOR B=1 TO 6
0050       FOR C=1 TO 6
0060          IF A+B+C<>N GOTO 0090
0070          LET K=K+1
0080          PRINT A;B;C
0090       NEXT C
0100    NEXT B
0110 NEXT A
0120 PRINT N;" CAN OCCUR IN ";K;" DIFFERENT WAYS"
0130 END


RUN
? 13
  1   6   6
  2   5   6
  2   6   5
  3   4   6
  3   5   5
  3   6   4
  4   3   6
  4   4   5
  4   5   4
  4   6   3
  5   2   6
  5   3   5
  5   4   4
  5   5   3
  5   6   2
  6   1   6
  6   2   5
  6   3   4
  6   4   3
  6   5   2
  6   6   1
 13   CAN OCCUR IN   21   DIFFERENT WAYS

*READY
```

It is possible to add two lines to speed up the program:

42 IF $A+B> = N$ THEN 110
54 IF $A+B+C>N$ THEN 100

Why will these speed it up?

Format control by the TAB function

So far, control of the format of the print-out of results from a program has been
by the use of commas, semi-colons and quotation marks. It is possible to exercise
greater control over the format in a PRINT statement by the use of the TAB
function. The TAB function moves the print head to the appropriate position
before printing the next character. For example:

```
LIST
0010 LET A=23
0020 LET B=76.35
0030 LET C=100.34
0040 LET D=345.21
0050 PRINT A; TAB (10);B; TAB (20);C; TAB (45);D
0060 END


RUN
 23          76.35      100.34                          345.21

*READY
```

Similarly, text can be started at any desired position of the carriage. The TAB
function is also useful to print rough graphs by using TAB (X) where X is
calculated within the program. Indeed X may be any valid expression. The
value of this expression is truncated since printing can only take place in integer
steps.

Clearly, there is an upper limit to the position to which the carriage can be
moved (usually 72) and so it may be necessary to scale down the carriage move-
ment. It is usually necessary to calculate the maximum value of the expression
it is desired to plot and to scale down accordingly. Although negative positions
cannot be used, it is always possible to move the axis to the centre of the page.
The only control down the page is by suppressing or adding line-feeds as
described in Chapter 3.

Example

Plot the graph of $y = x^2 + 3$ for values of x between 0 and 7.

```
LIST
0005 PRINT "--------------------Y AXIS--------------------------"
0010 FOR X=0 TO 7 STEP .5
0020    LET Y=X↑2+3
0030    PRINT "!"; TAB (Y);"+"
0040 NEXT X
0050 END

RUN
--------------------Y AXIS--------------------------
!   +
!   +
!    +
!     +
!      +
!       +
!        +
!         +
!          +
!           +
!            +
!             +
!              +
!               +
!                +

*READY
```

Problems 4B

4B.1 Write a program to plot sine and cosine functions.

4B.2 Write a program to plot a graph of $y = x^3 + 2x + 3$.

4B.3 Write a program to draw graphs of $y = 3x + 6$ and $y = x + 15$ on the same axes.

4B.4 Write a program which accepts Arabic numerals and prints out the equivalent Roman numerals.

4B.5 Write a program to print out a large circle.

4B.6 Write a program to print a large letter H, 9 print lines high and 9 print positions wide.

Arrays

When we wish to store information it is often convenient to form a list or an ARRAY of the data. For example, a milkman could note down the amount of milk required for each house in a street in an array such as

$(1, 6, 2, 3, 1, 0, 4, \ldots)$ where the first number refers to house one, the second number to house two, and so on.

We can call the whole array A and the single elements in the array are referred to as

$A(1)$, $A(2)$, $A(3)$, ... etc. respectively.

We can also refer to the Nth element in the array. This is called $A(N)$ where N is a positive whole number.

In the array above;
$$A(3) = 2$$
$$A(6) = 0$$
and, if $N = 4$, $A(N) = 3$.

This notation is available in BASIC as an extension of the simple variables used in previous chapters. The subscripts, $1, 2, 3, \ldots N, \ldots$ are often controlled in a FOR loop.

When an array is to be used, a DIMENSION statement, giving the maximum number of elements in the array, must be included to reserve space in the store.

e.g. DIM $A(15)$, $B(20)$.

Example

The milkman's sales in a street of 10 houses on one day are to be totalled. The program SALES shows how this may be done.

Flowchart for program SALES

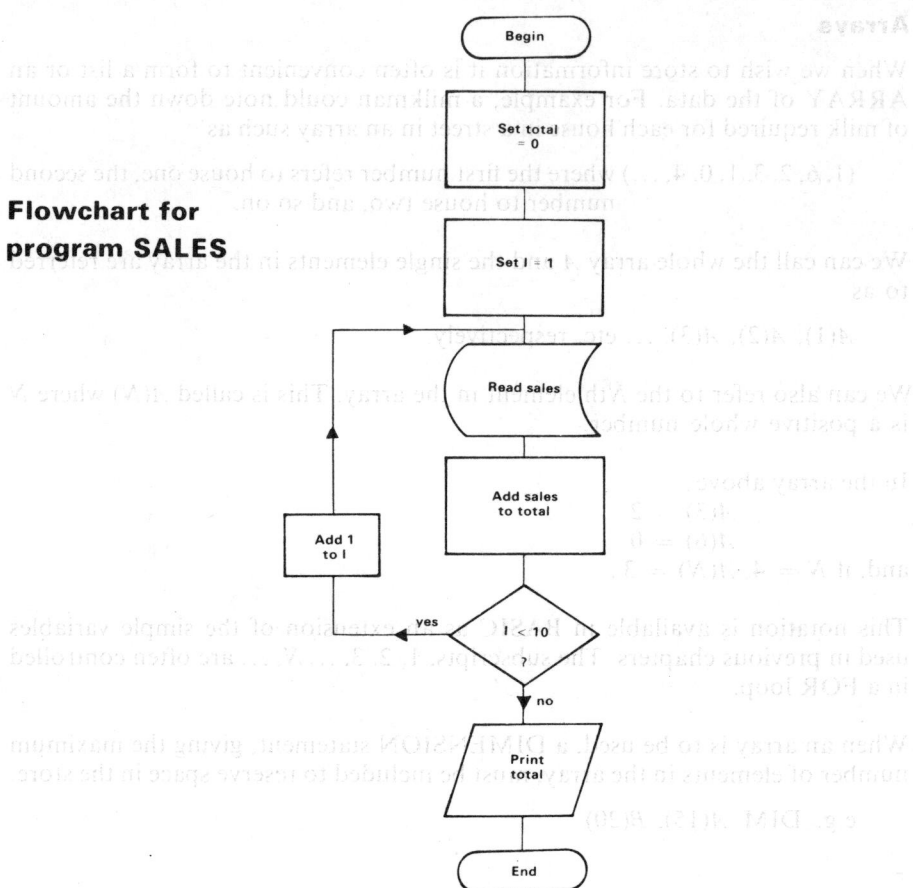

Program 'SALES'

```
LIST
0010 DIM S[10]
0020 LET T=0
0030 FOR I=1 TO 10
0040    READ S[I]
0050    LET T=T+S[I]
0060 NEXT I
0070 PRINT "TOTAL SALES =";T
0080 DATA 1, 2, 3, 2, 1, 2, 1, 1, 2, 1
0090 END


RUN
TOTAL SALES = 16

*READY
```

The milkman will produce 7 sales arrays during a week and if these are all put in DATA statements it is possible to add items to produce a new array of 10 items, the total sales for each house. The program MILK shows how this can be done.

**Flowchart for
program MILK**

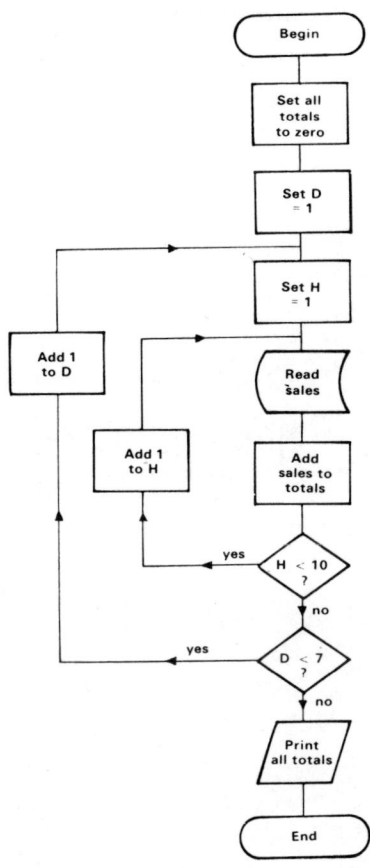

Program 'MILK'

```
LIST
0010 DIM D[7],H[10],T[10]
0020 FOR I=1 TO 10
0030    LET T[I]=0
0040 NEXT I
0060 FOR D=1 TO 7
0070    FOR H=1 TO 10
0080       READ S[H]
0090       LET T[H]=T[H]+S[H]
0100    NEXT H
0110 NEXT D
0120 FOR H=1 TO 10
0130    PRINT T[H];
0140 NEXT H
0150 DATA  1, 2, 3, 2, 1, 2, 1, 1, 2, 1
0151 DATA  1, 2, 2, 1, 2, 1, 1, 0, 1, 0
0152 DATA  0, 2, 5, 2, 1, 1, 1, 0, 2, 2
0153 DATA  1, 2, 2, 2, 2, 1, 1, 1, 0, 1
0154 DATA  2, 1, 2, 1, 1, 1, 2, 2, 2, 1
0155 DATA  1, 2, 1, 2, 2, 2, 2, 2, 1, 0
0156 DATA  1, 2, 2, 2, 1, 1, 1, 2, 0, 1
0160 END


RUN
 7  13  17  12  10  9  9  8  8  6
*READY
```

Lists

Most BASIC systems allow the creation of a list of names. For example, the milkman may list the occupants of the houses in a street:

(G. JONES, THOMAS, WILLIAMS, DAVIS, PRICE, F. JONES, ...)

This 'string array' may be referred to in BASIC with a single variable name and, as with numeric arrays, each item in the array can be referred to by the use of a subscript. If the above array has the name $N\$$ then

$$N\$(2) = \text{``THOMAS''}$$
$$N\$(5) = \text{``PRICE''}$$

and, if $C = 4$, $N\$(C) = \text{``DAVIS''}$

The number of names in the array must be stated in a DIM statement in the program. It is probable that the number of characters in each name will be limited. The exact limit will be dependent on the computer system.

Note that the string array facility will only be available on those systems which do not allow direct access to the individual characters within a string.

Also note that the use of the DIM statement here is different from that of systems which require each string variable to be dimensioned.

The use of these string arrays is shown in the program PAIRS which creates a list of six names and then prints out all possible combinations of two names from the list.

The program TROTA, of chapter 3, performs a similar, though more limited, function to PAIRS. This may be rewritten more neatly using a string array – writing this is left as an exercise for the reader.

LIST

PAIRS   15:22   G265 B 01/08/72

```
10  DIM A£(6)
20  FOR I=1 TO 6
30  READ A£(I)
40  NEXT I
50  FOR I=1 TO 5
60  FOR J=I+1 TO 6
70  PRINT A£(I),A£(J)
80  NEXT J
90  NEXT I
100 DATA ALAN,BRIAN,JOHN,PETER,MICHAEL,DAVID
110 END
```

RUN

PAIRS   15:23   G265 B 01/08/72

```
ALAN             BRIAN
ALAN             JOHN
ALAN           * PETER
ALAN             MICHAEL
ALAN             DAVID
BRIAN            JOHN
BRIAN            PETER
BRIAN            MICHAEL
BRIAN            DAVID
JOHN             PETER
JOHN             MICHAEL
JOHN             DAVID
PETER            MICHAEL
PETER            DAVID
MICHAEL          DAVID
```

Problems 4C

4C.1   Extend the milkman's sales program to print also the total sales each day.

4C.2   Given a list of numbers write a program to find the largest and the smallest.

4C.3   Given a list of numbers write a program to count the number of times each one occurs. A format for output could be:

aa OCCURS *xx* TIMES
bb OCCURS *yy* TIMES etc.

4C.4   Extend the previous program to select the most frequently occuring number. This is known as the mode of the set of numbers.

4C.5   The attendance register for a 10 day course is taken each day and appears as a list of zeros and ones corresponding to the list of participants. If there were 12 people on the course, a day's register might look like this: (1, 1, 1, 0, 0, 1, 1, 0, 1, 0, 1, 1). Write a program which gives the total present each day and the number of absences of each participant during the course.

4C.6   A farmer rears ducks and geese. Each goose requires twice the space of a duck and the farmer has space for 140 ducks. However, a local bye-law restricts him to a total of 100 birds. The cost of rearing a duck is 60p and of a goose 80p. They can be sold for 130p and 200p respectively. How many of each bird should be kept to maximise his profit?

Summary of the main points of Chapter Four

A group of instructions which are to be obeyed a number of times can be enclosed in a FOR . . . NEXT loop. The general form of the FOR statement is:

FOR variable $=$ expression TO expression STEP expression.

For example:

FOR $X = 3*A$ TO 1 STEP -1.

If step is omitted, the control variable is taken to be 1.
For example:

FOR $I = 3$ TO 7 I successively takes the values 3, 4, 5, 6, 7.

Every FOR statement must have a corresponding NEXT statement. Loops may be placed inside one another and it is permissible to jump out of a loop which contains an IF statement.

Format control may be exercised using the TAB(X) function. X may be a constant, variable or expression.

The elements or items in a list can be referenced by the use of subscripted variables. The Nth item in an array, A, is referred to as $A(N)$. A DIMension statement is required to allocate storage for each array used. For example:

10 DIM $A(12)$, $X(20)$.

Many systems allow string as well as numeric arrays.

Chapter 5

Numerical Methods

Iterative Methods

On meeting the various functions mentioned in Chapter 2, you may have wondered how the computer can calculate, say, the square root of a number, or the sine or cosine of an angle. In the case of the square root, one approach might be as follows:

Make a guess at the square root and square it. If the result is too small increase the guess by a small amount and square the new guess. If the result is too big, decrease the guess by a small amount and square the new guess. Continue this method until the result is as close to the answer as is required.

This is the basis of the program ROOT5A which finds better and better approximations to $\sqrt{5}$. This program follows and the corresponding flowchart is shown opposite.

```
ROOT5A     14:49     G265 B 02/08/72

10 REM****SQUARE ROOT****
15 LET G=2
20 LET I=.1
30 PRINT "INCREMENT IS "JI
40 LET G=G+I
50 PRINT G,G†2
60 IF G†2<5 THEN 40
70 IF G†2-5<.001 THEN 110
80 LET G=G-I
90 LET I=I/10
100 GOTO 30
110 PRINT "THE SQUARE ROOT OF 5 IS "JG
120 END
```

Notice that the use of a FOR – NEXT loop was not appropriate in this program because we do not know beforehand how many times the loop would be used. The program, in fact, makes certain assumptions. In particular, it is assumed that the intial value of the guess, G, is less than $\sqrt{5}$ and fairly close to it. If the program is generalised to accept as INPUT the initial guess, several modifications are necessary. Problems 5A contain one or two suggestions for developing this program.

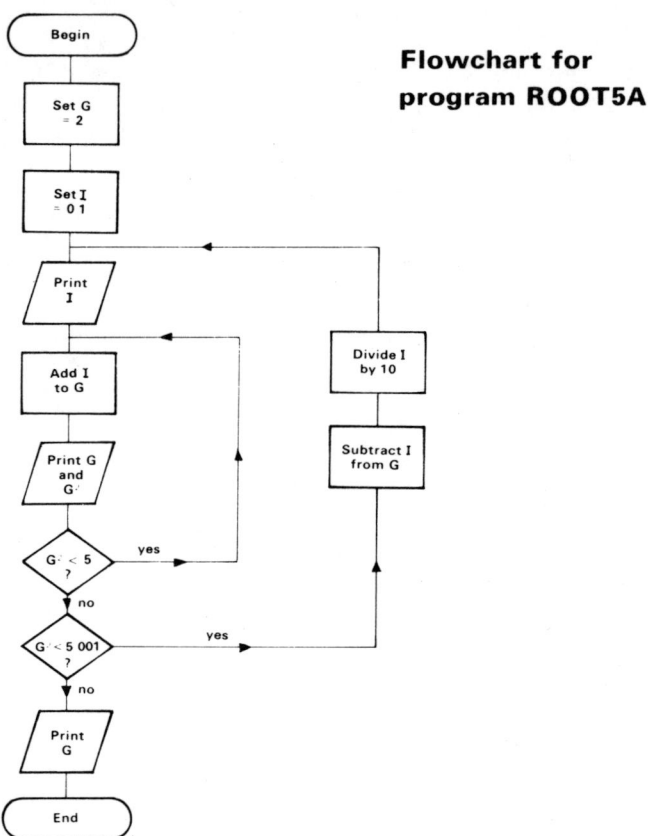

**Flowchart for
program ROOT5A**

Notes: G is used to denote 'guess'. I is used to denote 'increment'.

ROOT5A was an example of a program based on an iterative method – that is a method which is repeated a number of times to obtain results which get closer and closer to the required answer. This process is clearly seen in the printout of the computer run.

```
ROOT5A      14:49    G265 B 02/08/72

INCREMENT IS   .1
  2.1                    4.41
  2.2                    4.84
  2.3                    5.29
INCREMENT IS   .01
  2.21                   4.8841
  2.22                   4.9284
  2.23                   4.9729
  2.24                   5.0176
INCREMENT IS   .001
  2.231                  4.97736
  2.232                  4.98182
  2.233                  4.98629
  2.234                  4.99076
  2.235                  4.99522
  2.236                  4.9997
  2.237                  5.00417
INCREMENT IS   .0001
  2.2361                 5.00014
THE SQUARE ROOT OF 5 IS   2.2361
```

ROOT5A does not exhibit one usual aspect of an iterative process, namely an iteration formula. The next example shows what this is and how it is obtained.

If we now look at finding the square root of 5 in a geometrical way, it is equivalent to finding the side of a square whose area is 5 square units.

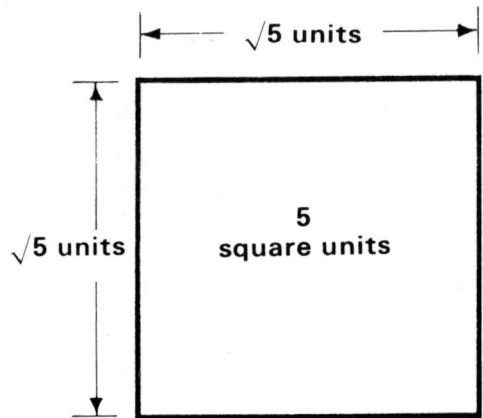

If we make a guess of 1 unit for the side, and adapt the figure to have an area of 5 square units the second side must be 5 units $(5 \div 1)$.

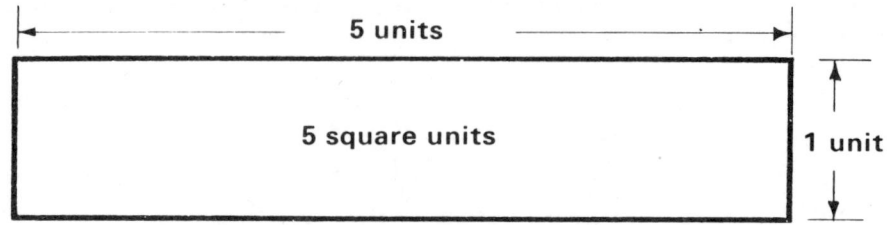

Now if one side is too small for $\sqrt{5}$, the other will be too large, and we may take the average of the two sides as a better estimate, $(1+5) \div 2 = 3$ units. We now use 3 as the first side of our figure and calculate the second side to be $5 \div 3 = 1\cdot667$.

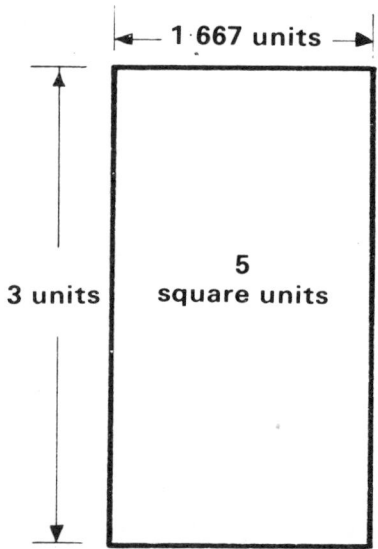

A better estimate of $\sqrt{5}$ is then $(3+1\cdot667) \div 2 = 2\cdot333$ and this is used as the first side of our next figure, and so on.

If we use N for the new estimate, our iteration formula is $N = \frac{1}{2}(E + 5/E)$; where E is the old estimate. Notice that it does not matter whether our old estimate is too large or too small, the new estimate is obtained from the same formula, and is always an improvement – unless, of course, our previous estimate was exactly the correct result.

This raises the question of when to stop our iterative procedure. Our first thought might be to stop when the new estimate and old estimate are exactly the same – but will this ever happen? In practice it is usual to stop the iteration when the difference between the new and previous estimates is as small as is required for the accuracy of the square root. A flowchart is given below, and a program with some typical printout follows.

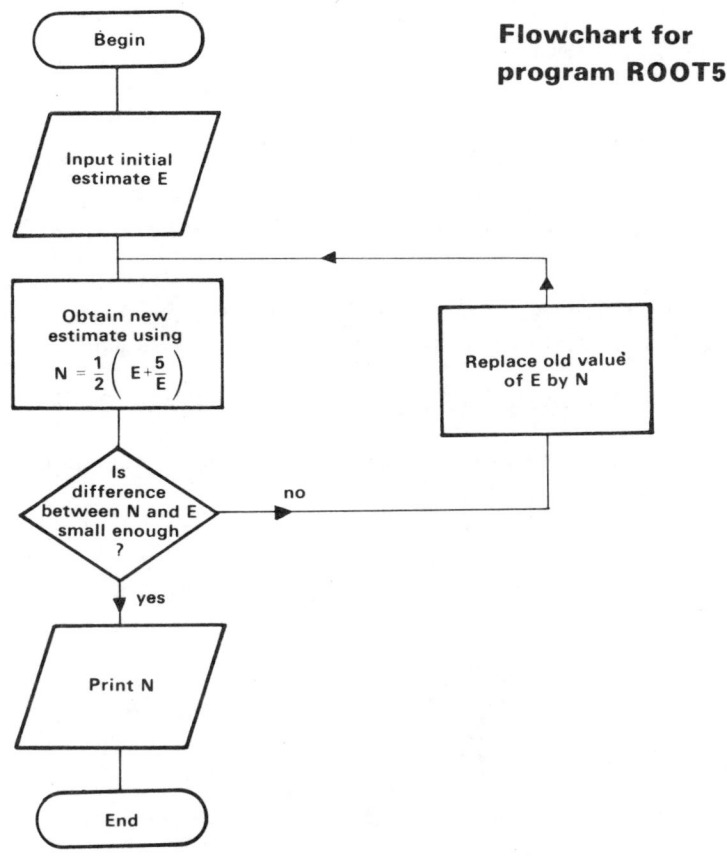

Flowchart for program ROOT5

```
ROOTS        14:54    G265 B 02/06/72

10 REM***ROOTS***
11 INPUT E
15 LET N=.5*(E+5/E)
20 PRINT N
25 IF ABS(N-E)<.0001 THEN 40
30 LET E=N
35 GOTO 15
40 PRINT "THE SQUARE ROOT OF 5 IS ";N
50 END

RUN



ROOTS        14:54    G265 B 02/06/72

? 1
 3
 2.33333
 2.2361
 2.23607
 2.23607
THE SQUARE ROOT OF 5 IS  2.23607
```

Notice the use of the ABS function, mentioned in Chapter 2, when programming the question 'Is the difference between N and E small enough?'.

In statement 30, the value of E is replaced by the value of N.

Notice in the following printout how even a ridiculous first estimate of 100 still gets the square root quite quickly.

```
ROOTS        14:55    G265 B 02/06/72

? 100
 50.025
 25.0625
 12.631
 6.51342
 3.64053
 2.50698
 2.25071
 2.23612
 2.23607
THE SQUARE ROOT OF 5 IS  2.23607
```

Problems 5A

5A.1 Adapt the program ROOT5A so that it will find the square root of any number. The number whose square root is to be found should be input, together with the initial guess and the accuracy required in the result.

5A.2 If you try to find the square root of a large number using the method of ROOT5A, an initial increment of 0·1 will mean that a great deal of time is taken before the root is found. Experiment with different starting values of the increment according to the size of the number whose square root is required. Write a program which decides its own first increment and its own first guess at the square root.

5A.3 Write a program to find a cube root of a number. You can start by trying to find the side of a cube whose volume is the number whose cube root you wish to find. If we put the solid on a square base of side G then the height of the solid must be N/G^2, where N is the volume of the solid. Now we take the average again to obtain a better guess of $\frac{1}{2}(G + N/G^2)$.

5A.4 Write a program which will find the largest value of the expression $3 + 5x - x^2$ in the range $x = 0$ to 4. Start by calculating the value of the expression when $x = 0$ and increase x by a small amount and again calculate the value of the expression. This is continued until the value of the expression has not increased when x has been increased. At this stage you can go back to the previous value of x and increase it by a smaller amount, and so on, in a similar way to the program ROOT5A.

5A.5 Use the TAB function to plot a graph of the various estimates in an iterative process. This will mean that every time a new estimate has been obtained the program will not print out its value, but will contain an instruction for the teleprinter to TAB across the value of the estimate and then to print a '*'. Remember that if the estimate is a small number it is possible to use an instruction such as PRINT TAB (10*G); "*".

5A.6 In order to solve the quadratic equation $x^2 + 5x - 8 = 0$ it is possible to use an iterative method. If a guess is made at a solution then a better guess is given by

$$\frac{8}{5 + \text{old guess}}$$

Use this iteration formula in a program to find a solution of the equation. Does the initial guess have any effect on the solution obtained? Experiment with different starting guesses.

User-defined functions

The functions defined in Chapter 2, for example SIN(X) and LOG(X), all require quite complex procedures for their calculation. The example we have just considered, on SQR(X), is a fairly simple one. The computer does not look up the values of such functions in tables! The values may well be calculated by a built-in sub-program similar to the ones we used for finding the square root, although it is likely that more sophisticated methods would be used.

The computer cannot carry built-in sub-programs for all possible functions required by users; hence you may need to write your own sub-programs such as the square root one above. If the function is a fairly simple one, so that it can be written down in a single statement, then BASIC has a special way of allowing this to be done. For example, suppose we wish to tabulate values of the expression

$$3x^3 + 2x^2 + 4$$

for various values of x, and then plot these values. This will mean that the program uses

$$X \uparrow 2*(3*X+2)+4$$

a number of times in its statements. By inserting the statement

$$\text{DEF FNA}(X) = X \uparrow 2*(3*X+2)+4$$

at the start of the program, we can then simply refer to FNA(X) at any stage during the program and the computer will calculate the value of $X \uparrow 2*(3*X+2)$ $+4$, using the current value of X, and use it in place of FNA(X). The program and printout shown should make clear the way in which such a statement can be used.

```
PLOTFN      14:58      G265 B 02/08/72

10 DEF FNY(X)=X↑2*(3*X+2)+4
20 FOR X=-1 TO 2 STEP 0.2
30 PRINT X;FNY(X)
40 NEXT X
50 FOR X=-1 TO 2 STEP 0.2
60 PRINT "*";TAB(FNY(X));"*"
70 NEXT X
80 END
```

Notice, in the printout, that although the program is going through values of x in steps of 0·2 from -1 to $+2$, it seems that x does not take exactly the value zero, but takes the value $-·00000000186265$. The reason is that the computer does not hold numbers in base 10, but in some other base, perhaps base two or base eight. Consequently, rounding errors sometimes occur, giving unusual results such as this one.

```
PLOTFN      14:59     G265 B 02/08/72

 -1   3
 -.8        3.744
 -.6        4.072
 -.4        4.128
 -.2        4.056
 -1.86265E-09      4
  .2        4.104
  .4        4.512
  .6        5.368
  .8        6.816
 1.         9.
 1.2       12.064
 1.4       16.152
 1.6       21.408
 1.8       27.976
 2.        36.
  *      *
  *      *
  *         *
  *         *
  *         *
  *         *
  *         *
  *         *
  *           *
  *             *
  *               *
  *                 *
  *                   *
  *                     *
  *                         *
  *
```

The general form of the statement is

    DEF FNα (variable) = any expression containing the variable

where α is any letter of the alphabet. There are, therefore, 26 of these functions that may be defined in any one program. The following are all valid uses of the statement –

    DEF FNC(B) = $1·414*B - 1·732*B \uparrow 2$
    DEF FNT(A) = SQR($B \uparrow 2 - 4*A*C$)
    DEF FNZ(B) = SQR($A \uparrow 2 + B \uparrow 2$).

It is possible to make use of one user-defined function when defining a further function, so that the following two statements are a correct use of the method:

10 DEF FND(X) $=$ $X \uparrow 2 - 2*X + 6$

. . .

. . .

60 DEF FNK(X) $=$ FND(X) $\uparrow 2 + 3*$FND(X) $+4.$

It should be made clear that these are not permanent functions like the SQR and LOG functions; they can be used only in the program in which they are defined.

Area under a graph

It may seem strange at first sight that a computer can calculate the area under a graph. There are a number of methods, all of them approximate, but in a similar way to that used to improve the results obtained by iterative methods, the area can be obtained to greater degrees of accuracy.

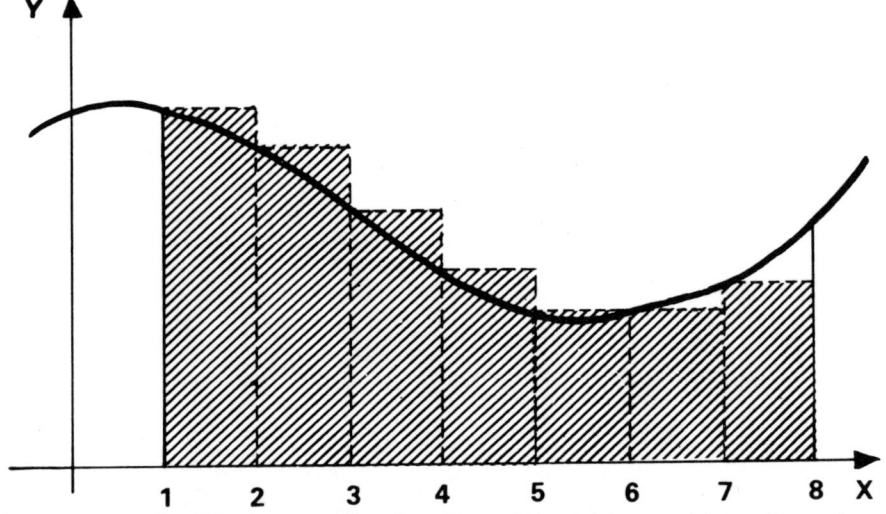

If we want to find the area under the curve shown, between the points where $x = 1$ and $x = 8$, the area is divided up as indicated. The divisions are normally of equal width, but the width does not have to be one unit. In general, the greater the number of divisions the more accurate will be the result. The areas of the rectangles shaded in the figure are found and added up, and the sum is used as an approximate value for the area under the curve. Sometimes the area of the rectangle will be larger than the corresponding area under the curve and sometimes the area of the rectangle will be smaller.

To calculate the area of the first rectangle, the value of y is calculated when $x = 1$, and this is multiplied by the width of a division. This is added on to a running total of area. The value of x is increased by the width of a division, a check is made to see if the final value of x (8) has been reached and, if not, a new value of y is calculated, a new rectangle area is found and added on to the running total. If after increasing the value of x, it is found that the final value of x has been reached, the total area found so far is printed out.

Let us apply this approach to find the area of one quarter of a circle.

The method used is to find the area under the curve $y = \sqrt{(1 - x^2)}$ between $x = 0$ and $x = 1$. The flowchart and program follow.

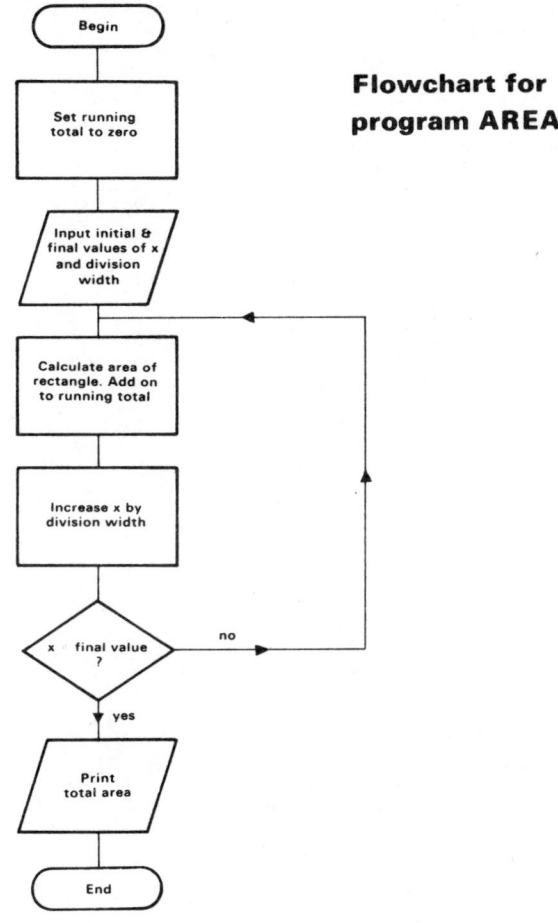

Flowchart for program AREA

```
AREA          15:02     G265 B 02/08/72

10  DEF FNY(X)=SQR(1-X↑2)
20  INPUT I,F,D
30  LET A=0
40  LET X=I
50  LET A=A+D*FNY(X)
60  LET X=X+D
70  IF X<F THEN 50
80  PRINT "AREA IS ";A
90  END
```

Three computer runs of this program follow and the large increase in computer time in the final printout should be noted. This is one disadvantage of using a very small division width. Another disadvantage is that the result may not be very reliable because of a very large number of small 'round off' errors being added together during the program.

```
RUN


AREA          15:02     G265 B 02/08/72

? 0,1,0.1
AREA IS  .826137

USED       2.50 UNITS.
RUN


AREA          15:03     G265 B 02/08/72

? 0,1,0.01
AREA IS  .790106

USED       3.00 UNITS.
RUN


AREA          15:04     G265 B 02/08/72

? 0,1,0.0001
AREA IS  .785446
```

There are other methods of finding the area under a graph, two of which are fairly simple extensions of the 'rectangle' method you have just met.

In the 'trapezium' method, the rectangles in the diagram on an earlier page are replaced by trapezia, as shown in the diagram below.

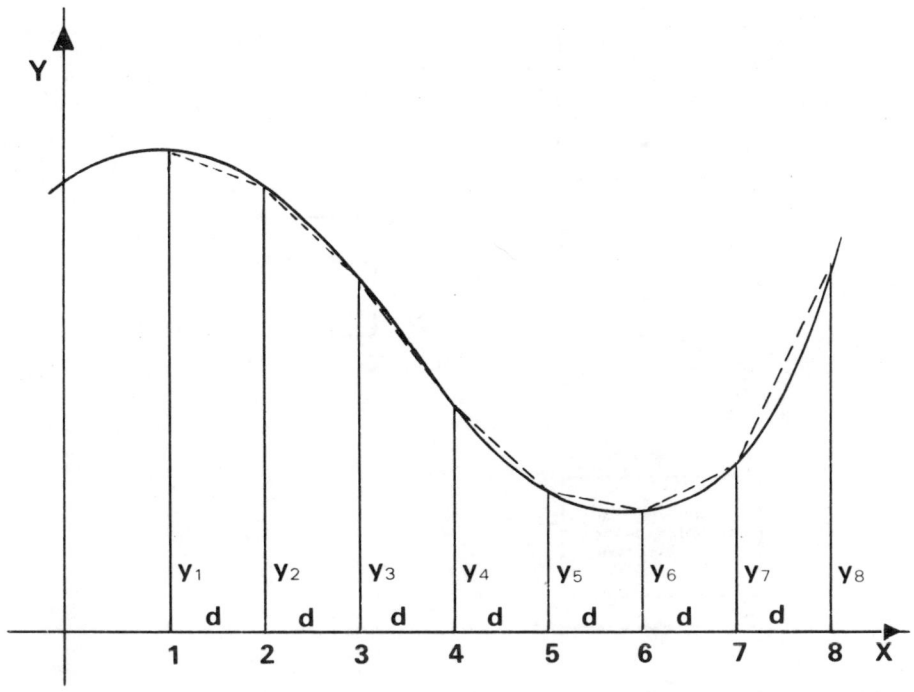

The area of a trapezium is found by taking the average of the two parallel sides and multiplying this by the distance between them. In the case of the first trapezium in the diagram, this gives:

$$d \times \tfrac{1}{2}(y_1 + y_2)$$

and when all the areas of the trapezia are added together we obtain:

$$d \times (\tfrac{1}{2}y_1 + y_2 + y_3 + \ldots + y_7 + \tfrac{1}{2}y_8).$$

A flowchart follows, but the program is left as an exercise for the reader.

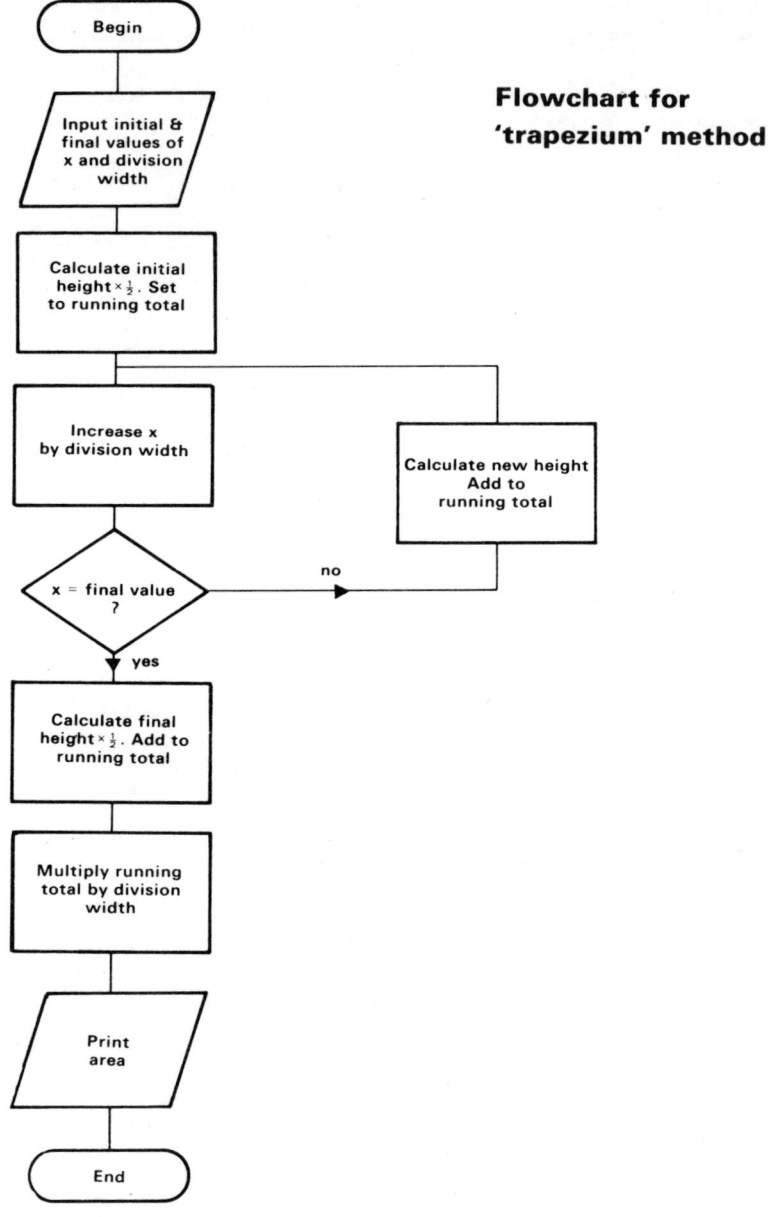

Flowchart for 'trapezium' method

In the 'mid-point' method, instead of taking the height of the curve at the left-hand end of the division as the height of the rectangle, we go to the point half-way through the division and use the height of the curve there as the height of the rectangle. The diagram below shows what happens.

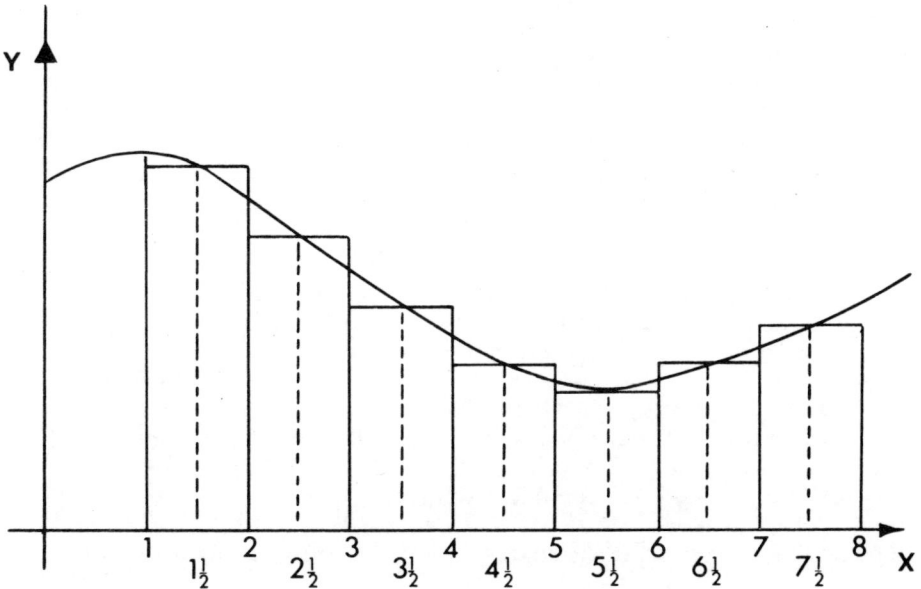

The program which uses this method is very similar to the program for the rectangle method, and the flowchart and program are left as an exercise for the reader.

Problems

5B.1 Write a program to calculate x^n where x and n are to be input and n is a whole number.

5B.2 Write a program which will print out a list of the numbers from 1 to 10, together with their factorials.

5B.3 Find the area of a circle of radius one unit
a) using the rectangle method
b) using the trapezium method
c) using the mid-point method
using the same division width. Compare the results to see which method seems to give the best answer.

5B.4 Plot a graph of the function $x^2 + x - 6$ for values of x from -5 to $+5$. Include in your print out an indication of the x-axis. Note that if the graph goes below the axis the method of printing the axis and the point will differ from that when the graph is above the axis.

5B.5 Write a program which will plot the graphs of two functions at the same time, using '*' for the first and '+' for the second. The problems encountered in 5B.4 when printing the axis and the graph arises here also, but in a slightly more complicated form.

5B.6 One way to calculate the sine of an angle $x°$ is to use the series

$$\sin x° = y - \frac{y^3}{3!} + \frac{y^5}{5!} - \frac{y^7}{7!} + \ldots$$

where $y = \Pi x / 180$. The more terms of the series that are taken, the more accurate will be the result. Write a program which calculates the sine of an angle using this method and compare your results with the SIN function available on the computer you are using.

Chapter 6

Procedures and Subroutines

Sorting

The problem of arranging a set of numbers into a particular order is one which frequently occurs in computing. In Chapter 2, using the IF statement, a procedure was written for arranging two numbers in order. Two distinct approaches to this are shown in the flowcharts opposite.

There appears to be little to choose between these approaches to this simple problem. However, try to draw a flowchart, based on the first solution, which will allow you to sort 3 numbers into ascending order. You will find that it becomes complicated quite quickly, and this is still a trivial problem!

Real problems for sorting a list of numbers would be impossible to solve using this method. A great deal of effort has been applied to finding simple iterative procedures for computer sorting. The second flowchart provides us with a step towards a general solution of this problem.

This effectively prints out the numbers a and b in ascending order, but only involves one PRINT statement. If a is greater than b the procedure 'swops' the values using a third variable c as an intermediate 'carrier'. Check this with actual values, for example of $a = 6$ and $b = 3$:

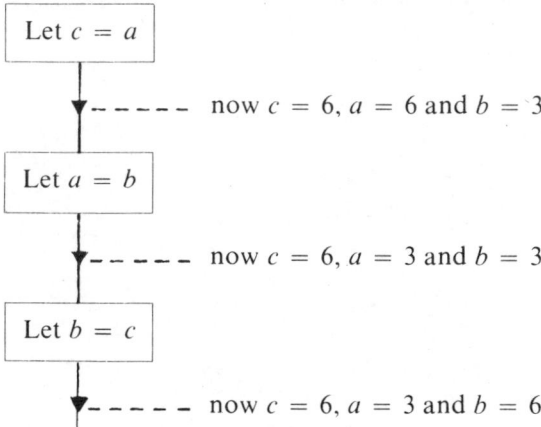

and the values of a and b have been changed over.

The first flowchart uses different PRINT instructions, the second flowchart adapts the values of *a* and *b* to fit the one PRINT instruction. You should check what happens if the values of *a* and *b* are equal at the start of the flowchart.

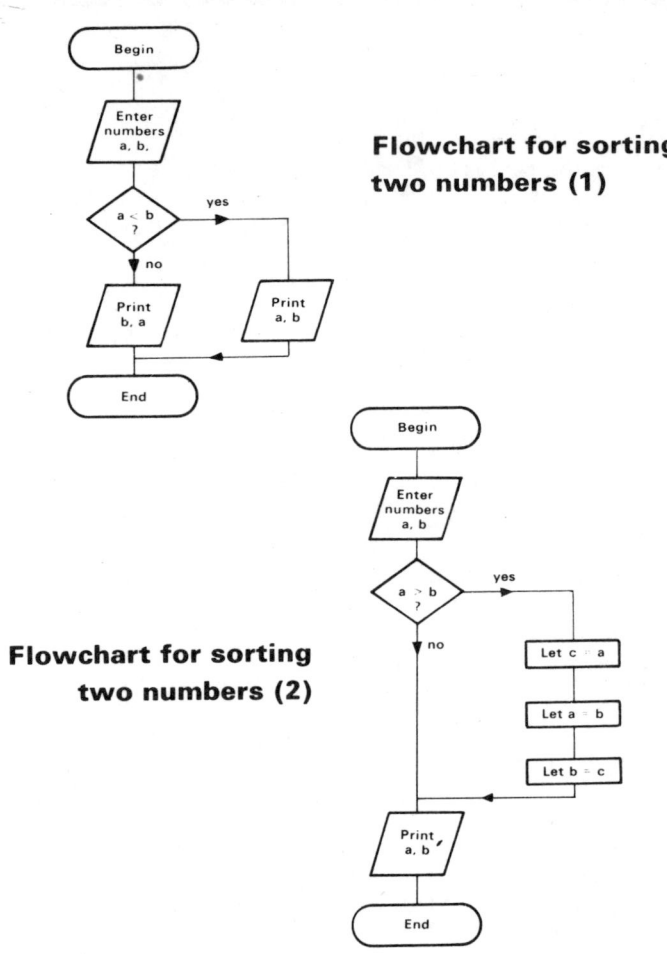

Flowchart for sorting two numbers (1)

Flowchart for sorting two numbers (2)

Sorting a list of numbers

Suppose that the numbers we have to sort are stored in locations A, B, C, D, E. The method we shall use has the following steps:

STEP 1   Inspect contents of A and B, if $A > B$ swop the contents

STEP 2   Inspect contents of B and C, if $B > C$ swop the contents

STEP 3   Inspect contents of C and D, if $C > D$ swop the contents

STEP 4   Inspect contents of D and E, if $D > E$ swop the contents

Having arrived at the end of the list, are the numbers contained in A, B, C, D and E in order? Probably not, and so we go back to STEP 1 and repeat the procedure. How many times do we have to go through the procedure of scanning the list to be certain that the numbers are all in order? Well, that depends on how near to the correct order the numbers were in the first place. One sure way of being certain that the ordering is completed is to count the number of swops made in one complete scan of the list. If there are no swops then the list must be in order.

The example opposite shows how this procedure works for a sample set of numbers.

Notice that although the numbers are in fact in order at the end of the third scan, the computer would have no way of knowing this other than by scanning the list again. The fourth scan must be made in order to find out that no more swops are necessary.

The contents of locations A, B, C, D, E, in that order, may now be printed out and the numbers will be in ascending order.

This method of applying a procedure over and over again until an end result has been achieved is a further example of iterative procedures which were introduced in Chapter Five.

Will this procedure handle a list containing two or more equal numbers?

```
           A  B  C  D  E
STEP 1: swop A, B    4  3  7  1  6   initial order
STEP 2: leave B, C   3  4  7  1  6   order after STEP 1
STEP 3: swop C, D    3  4  7  1  6   order after STEP 2
STEP 4: swop D, E    3  4  1  7  6   order after STEP 3
                     3  4  1  6  7   order at end of first scan
```

3 SWOPS MADE

```
STEP 1: leave A, B   3  4  1  6  7   order at start of second scan
STEP 2: swop B, C    3  4  1  6  7   order after STEP 1
STEP 3: leave C, D   3  1  4  6  7   order after STEP 2
STEP 4: leave D, E   3  1  4  6  7   order after STEP 3
                     3  1  4  6  7   order at end of second scan
```

1 SWOP MADE

```
STEP 1: swop A, B    3  1  4  6  7   order at start of third scan
STEP 2: leave B, C   1  3  4  6  7   order after STEP 1
STEP 3: leave C, D   1  3  4  6  7   order after STEP 2
STEP 4: leave D, E   1  3  4  6  7   order after STEP 3
                     1  3  4  6  7   order at end of third scan
```

1 SWOP MADE

```
STEP 1: leave A, B   1  3  4  6  7   order at start of fourth scan
STEP 2: leave B, C   1  3  4  6  7   order after STEP 1
STEP 3: leave C, D   1  3  4  6  7   order after STEP 2
STEP 4: leave D, E   1  3  4  6. 7   order after STEP 3
                     1  3  4  6  7   order at end of fourth scan
```

0 SWOPS MADE   **– STOP –**

This procedure is the basis of the following flowchart for the program SWOPST shown opposite.

Flowchart for program SWOPST

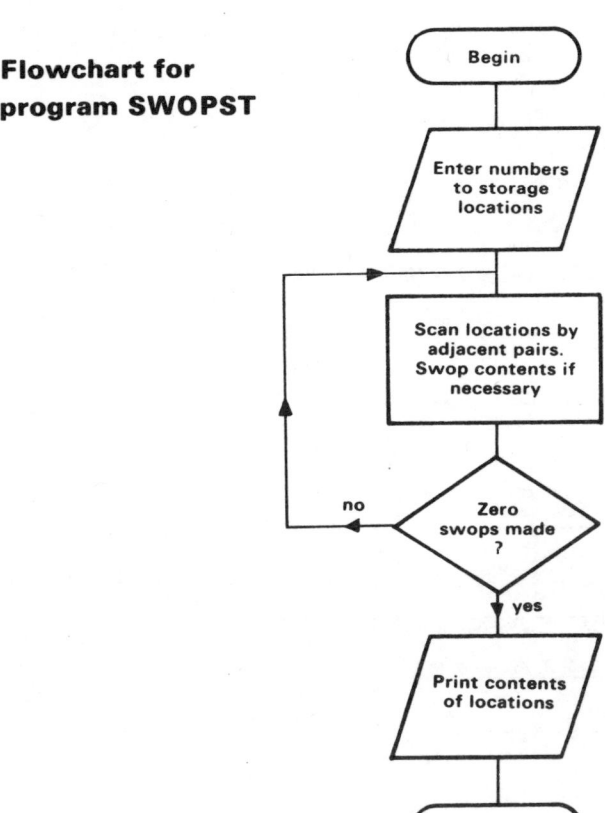

The list of numbers forms an array and the numbers, the elements of the array, are handled by the use of subscripts under the control of a series of FOR loops. The annotation to the program indicates this.

It is only because of the subscript facility that the scanning and necessary swopping can be performed so elegantly. This also means that it would be quite easy to modify the program to accept a list of N numbers and to sort these.

The counter, S, keeps a note of the swops made and is tested at the end of each scan. It is set to zero prior to the next scan.

If it is desired to have the numbers printed in descending order, you may either change statement 140 to read

140 FOR $I = 8$ TO 1 STEP -1

or change statement 70 to read

70 IF $N(J) > = N(J+1)$ THEN 120.

```
LIST
SWOPST

10    DIM N[10]                                      ⎫
20    FOR I=1 TO 8                                   ⎬  loop to enter numbers to
30    READ N[I]                                      ⎪  storage locations
40    NEXT I                                         ⎭
50    LET S=0
60    FOR J=1 TO 7                                   ⎫
70    IF N[J] <= N[J+1] THEN 120                     ⎪
80    LET C=N[J]          ⎫                          ⎪
90    LET N[J]=N[J+1]     ⎬ swops contents of 2 loca-⎪  scans list of 8 locations
100   LET N[J+1]=C        ⎪ tions and increases swop ⎪
110   LET S=S+1           ⎭ count                    ⎪
120   NEXT J                                         ⎭
125   PRINT "END OF SCAN ";S;" SWOPS MADE"
130   IF   S>0 THEN 50
135   PRINT "ORDERED  LIST  FOLLOWS:-"
140   FOR I=1 TO 8                                   ⎫
150   PRINT N[I];                                    ⎬  loop to print numbers in
160   NEXT I                                         ⎭  ascending order
170   DATA 24,16,5,3,27,1,6,5
180   END


RUN
SWOPST   1533

END OF SCAN   6   SWOPS MADE
END OF SCAN   5   SWOPS MADE
END OF SCAN   4   SWOPS MADE
END OF SCAN   2   SWOPS MADE
END OF SCAN   1   SWOPS MADE
END OF SCAN   0   SWOPS MADE
ORDERED   LIST   FOLLOWS:-
 1   3   5   5   6   16   24   27
DONE AT   1533
```

Although the program **SWOPST** will certainly do the job of sorting numbers into order, it is rather wasteful of computer time. Consider the stages of a scan of a list of six numbers.

initial order	7	**14**	2	9	3	4
after 1st comparison	7	**14**	2	9	3	4
after 2nd comparison	7	2	**14**	9	3	4
after 3rd comparison	7	2	9	**14**	3	4
after 4th comparison	7	2	9	3	**14**	4
after 5th comparison	7	2	9	3	4	**14**

FIRST SCAN COMPLETE

Notice that the largest number in the list (14) occupies the last place. Notice too how the 14 has 'bubbled' through the list, giving the alternative name of 'bubble sort' for this method.

Now, knowing that the final storage location must hold the largest of the original set of numbers, there is no need to include this final location in the next scanning of the list. The next scan will place the second highest number in the original list in the next to the last storage location.

7	2	**9**	3	4	14
2	7	**9**	3	4	14
2	7	**9**	3	4	14
2	7	3	**9**	4	14
2	7	3	4	**9**	14

SECOND SCAN COMPLETE

The following scan may therefore omit the final **two** steps, and so on – the length of each scan being reduced by one step. This simple amendment to the program will considerably reduce the number of comparisons which have to be made.

Problems 6A

6A.1 Using the ideas given in the program in the text, write a program which finds the largest of a given list of numbers (or the smallest).

6A.2 If a set of numbers is arranged in order, from smallest to largest, the middle number (or the average of the two middle numbers if the set has an even number of members) is called the median. Write a program to print out the median of a list of numbers.

6A.3 Modify the program SWOPST so that the number of comparisons to be made is reduced, as described. Delete all printing statements (when you are sure the programs work) if you wish to compare this with the original program SWOPST. This deletion is necessary since printing takes up most of the connect time, swamping the processing time. In making the comparison, it is also necessary to use a larger set than the 8 elements of the SWOPST data.

6A.4 An alternative method of sorting is to note the first number in the list and to compare it with the rest in turn until a larger number is found. This larger number is now noted, and so on, until the end of the list is reached. Use this method in a program which finds the largest of a given set of numbers.

6A.5 If, in the method of 6A.4, the location which held the largest number in the list is now filled with the number 0, a further search can be made for the second largest number in the list. Write a program which prints out the largest three numbers in a given list of positive numbers, using this method.

6A.6 Extend the program in 6A.5 to print out the list of numbers in descending order. Is this method any quicker than the swop-sort method?

Subroutines

When solving major problems by computer it is normal to try to break down a single problem into a series of small ones and to write and test each part separately. This makes error detection, known as 'debugging', particularly of logical errors, much easier. This approach to solving problems is especially useful when a particular series of operations is used repeatedly.

When a large program is broken down into small parts, it is very helpful to someone looking at the program if notes are added to explain what is happening at various points. The REM statement described in Chapter 3, allows this to be done within a program.

In any major programming job good documentation is essential as many people may be involved in the original writing or in later modifications of the programs.

In BASIC, as in many other languages, it is possible to refer to part of a program as a SUBROUTINE. This is particularly valuable when a section of program is to be used a number of times within the same program. A feature of a subroutine is that it automatically returns to the appropriate point in the main program each time it has been used.

A flowchart which refers twice to a subroutine could be drawn as follows:

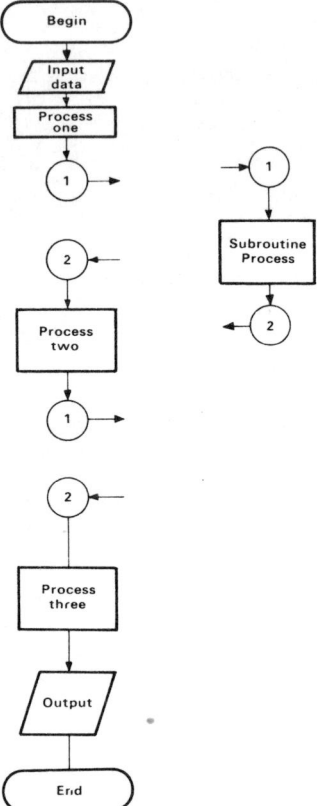

Note: To emphasise the repetition of the subroutine, it has only been represented once on the flowchart. This can result in ambiguity concerning the point of return and it is more usual to repeat the subroutine, as in the flowchart for the program SUBSRT later in this chapter.

The two BASIC statements involved in subroutine jumps are

GOSUB (statement number) which causes a jump to the statement number specified

and

RETURN which, used as the last statement in the subroutine, causes a return to the statement immediately following the GOSUB which caused the jump.

These statements are shown in the following skeleton program.

```
10
20
30
 .
 .
 .
70 GOSUB 200
80 REM FIRST RETURN FROM SUB TO HERE
90
 .
 .
 .
150 GOSUB 200
160 REM SECOND RETURN TO HERE
 .
 .
 .
190 STOP
200 REM THIS IS THE BEGINNING OF SUBROUTINE
210
 .
 .
 .
240 REM THE SUBR ENDS WITH NEXT STATEMENT
250 RETURN
260 END
```

Note here the use of STOP to avoid running into the subroutine unintentionally at the end of the main program. As indicated in Chapter 2, STOP is equivalent to GOTO n where n is the statement number of the END statement – in this case GOTO 260.

Let us now consider the use, as a subroutine, of one of this chapter's programs, SWOPST, to sort a list of numbers.

Flowchart for program SUBSRT

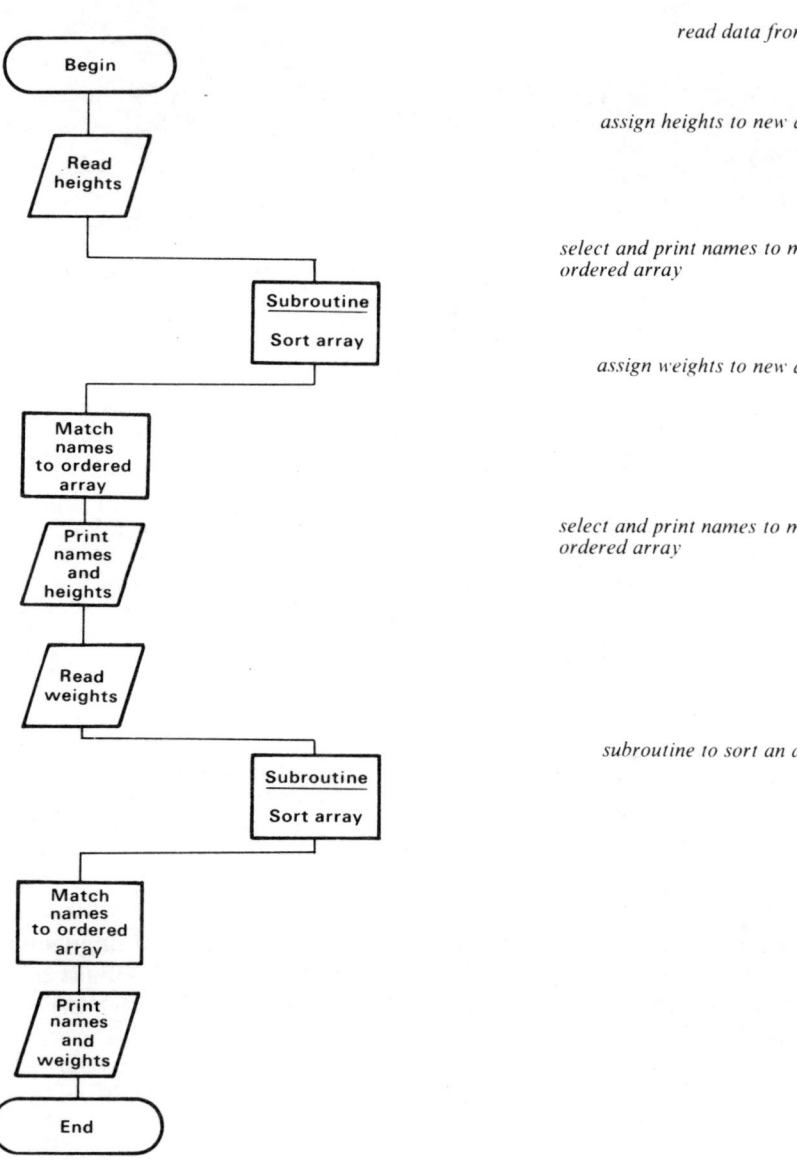

read data from file

assign heights to new array

select and print names to match ordered array

assign weights to new array

select and print names to match ordered array

subroutine to sort an array

```
    LIST
    SUBSRT

  5   DIM A$[10],S[20],H[20],W[20]
 10   LET N=-1
 20   LET N=N+1
 30   READ A$,H[N+1],W[N+1]
 40   IF A$ <> "END" THEN 20
 45   RESTORE
 50   FOR K=1 TO N
 60   LET S[K]=H[K]
 70   NEXT K
 80   GOSUB 500
 83   PRINT "NAME          HEIGHT(CMS)"
 85   FOR C=1 TO N
 90   FOR K=1 TO N
100   READ A$,H[K],W[K]
110   IF S[C]=H[K] THEN 120
115   NEXT K
120   PRINT A$,H[K]
130   RESTORE
140   NEXT C
150   FOR K=1 TO N
160   LET S[K]=W[K]
170   NEXT K
180   GOSUB 500
181   PRINT
182   PRINT
183   PRINT "NAME          WEIGHT(KGS)"
185   FOR C=1 TO N
190   FOR K=1 TO N
200   READ A$,H[K],W[K]
210   IF S[C]=W[K] THEN 220
215   NEXT K
220   PRINT A$,W[K]
230   RESTORE
240   NEXT C
490   STOP
500   LET C=0
505   FOR K=1 TO N-1
510   IF S[K]<S[K+1] THEN 540
520   NEXT K
530   GOTO 590
540   LET S=S[K]
550   LET S[K]=S[K+1]
560   LET S[K+1]=S
570   LET C=C+1
580   GOTO 520
590   IF C>0 THEN 500
600   RETURN
610   DATA "BROWN",200,80
615   DATA "SMITH",180,70
620   DATA "JONES",175,65.4
625   DATA "WILLIAMS",190,85
630   DATA "HARRIS",170,65
635   DATA "BLACK",185,71
640   DATA "KELLY",186,71.5
650   DATA "WARD",205,88.3
660   DATA "END",0,0
700   END
```

```
RUN
SUBSRT     1341

NAME              HEIGHT(CMS)
WARD                 205
BROWN                200
WILLIAMS             190
KELLY                186
BLACK                185
SMITH                180
JONES                175
HARRIS               170


NAME              WEIGHT(KGS)
WARD                 88.3
WILLIAMS             85
BROWN                80
KELLY                71.5
BLACK                71
SMITH                70
JONES                65.4
HARRIS               65

DONE AT    1342
```

Example

A series of DATA statements contains names of people, together with their heights and weights. The structure of this file is:

1st NAME   1st HEIGHT   1st WEIGHT
2nd NAME 2nd HEIGHT 2nd WEIGHT
  .
  .
  .
'END'   0   0

From this data file it is required to produce a printout of the names in a certain order:

1. so that the heights of the people are in order
2. so that the weights of the people are in order.

The subroutine (based on the program SWOPST) is written to sort an array of numbers, S. Before it can be used on the data file, the array, S, must first be created from the list of heights and second from the list of weights.

After the sorting of the first list is complete, a comparison with the unchanged height array allows the name associated with each height to be found and so printed out. This procedure is then repeated with the weight array.

The various stages in the process are shown in the flowchart which follows. These stages are indicated alongside the listing of the program SUBSRT.

It should be noted that the subroutine based on SWOPST does not permit equal values of the variable.

The program SUBSRT has been run on a system which requires each string variable to be dimensioned and which does not allow string arrays. A much shorter program is possible if string arrays are used.

Random numbers and simulation

If you throw a die, what number would you expect to show? If you toss a penny, would you expect it to land showing a head or a tail?

In each of these cases there is a certain chance of obtaining a particular result. For example, if you threw a die 600 times you would expect to find that a '5' occurred on *about* 100 occasions. For an individual throw, however, the chance of getting a particular score would be equal to the chance of getting any other score. In other words we can get a result between 1 and 6 at *RANDOM*.

Many problems in the world are governed by the rules of chance and in solving these the problems are often simulated on a computer. For example, a port authority may be trying to decide whether or not to build a new unloading berth. Now, the arrival of ships and lorries at a dock may not be completely random but there is a large element of chance on whether the ship was delayed by fog or some of the lorries delayed in a traffic jam. It is possible to simulate the arrival of ships and lorries at the berth on a computer and this will certainly be cheaper than building the berth to see if it is going to be economical.

In order to be able to simulate these chance events, the computer must be able to generate random numbers. In BASIC this facility is available using the RND function in which a number is chosen at random between 0 and 1. In fact, the numbers generated are not true random numbers and care should be taken if the program is re-run as the same set of numbers may be generated. Thus, if we write $Y = RND(X)$ Y takes on a value between 0 and 1. X can have any value. It is in fact a dummy number which may have some significance on some systems.

To show the use of the RND function, we will investigate the simulation of the game of snakes and ladders. We first need to be able to generate random integers in the range 1 to 6 to simulate the die. We will try various expressions involving $RND(X)$ in our search for the die simulator.

expression	*range and form of numbers*
$RND(X)$	Real numbers in the range 0 to 1
$6*RND(X)$	Real numbers in the range 0 to 6
$INT(6*RND(X))$	Integers in the range 0 to 5. Normally the range of $RND(X)$ excludes 1 and hence, on truncation, 6 is not included.
$INT(6*RND(X)+1)$	Integers in the range 1 to 6.

Having established a die simulator routine, we turn now to the snakes and ladders board. It is easiest to represent the squares of the board by the elements of an array. Thus, the squares of a 10 × 10 board are represented by an array, B, element $B(1)$ referring to square 1, element $B(2)$ to square 2, and so on.

When a player lands on a square there are three things that may happen to him.

1. he may climb a ladder and so advance N squares up the board
2. he may slide down a snake and so go back M squares down the board
3. he may stay where he is.

The elements of the array, B, will have values of $+N$, corresponding to a square containing the foot of a ladder, $-M$, corresponding to a square containing the head of a snake or Zero for a blank square. For example, the simple board shown in the figure would be represented by the array with elements:

$(0, +4, 0, -3, +3, 0, -4, 0, 0)$.

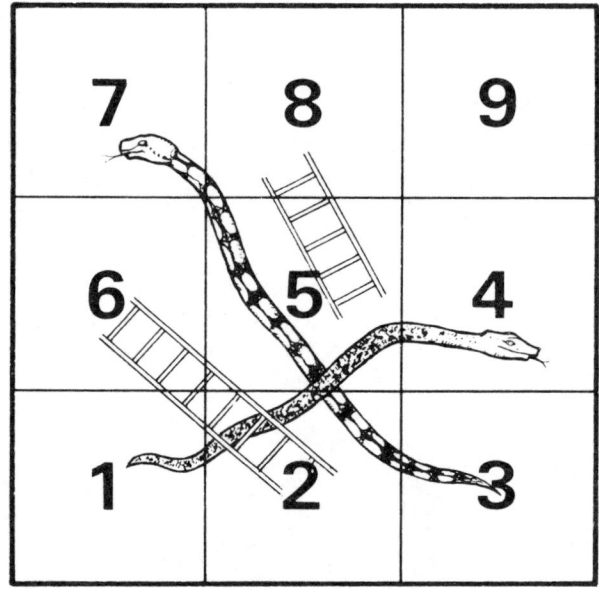

Each player has a counter telling him his current position and each move is a combination of an integer from the die routine and then the addition of the element from the array corresponding to the square on which he first landed.

Other rules of the game such as each player having to throw a 'six' to start or the possibility of two players occupying the same square must be decided by the program writer.

The particularly interesting feature about this form of the game is the ease with which the board can be changed. It is just necessary to change some elements of the array B.

Problems 6B

6B.1 Using the expression, derived in the chapter, for simulating a die, develop the program for the snakes and ladders game to be played by two players.

6B.2 For a single player, how many throws of the die, on average, are needed to traverse the board? How is this affected by the sum of the elements in the array which simulates the board? How important is the effect of changing the distribution of snakes and ladders on the board on the average numbers of throws to complete the game?

6B.3 We were able to simulate a single die quite easily as the chances of any score were equal. If we consider rolling two dice the chance of scoring a total of '3' is different from the chance of scoring a total of '8'. Write a program to simulate the rolling of two dice simultaneously.

6B.4 The expression which gives the probability of exactly I successes in N experiments when the probability of success of each individual experiment is P, is

$$\frac{N!}{I!(N-I)!} \times P^I(1-P)^{N-I}.$$

Use the program developed in problem 4A.2 for calculating factorials as a subroutine in a program to evaluate this expression for various values of N, I and P.

6B.5 Some BASIC systems have the function SGN(X) defined such that

if $Y = \text{SGN}(X)$, Y is set to 0   if $X = 0$
                           Y is set to $+1$ if $X > 0$
                           Y is set to -1 if $X < 0$.

If your system does not have this function, use the ABS(X) function in writing a subroutine to perform the same function as SGN(X).

6B.6 Using the simulation of the rolling of two dice, investigate the snakes and ladders game when players roll two dice for each move.

Chapter 7

File Handling

Storage of information

In computer systems, information may be stored on a variety of devices. So far, these devices have not been considered since one feature of BASIC – in common with most high level languages – is that the programmer is not concerned with the actual storage location. However, even in BASIC, if a lot of information – programs or data – has to be stored, it is necessary to consider the supporting storage available. The actual mechanism employed will differ in different systems but principally we are concerned with fundamental ideas. While trying to cover ideas common to many BASIC systems it is impossible to be exhaustive and so reference to the particular system manual will be necessary.

In order to reduce the amount of referencing, this chapter is structured so that the main ideas, problems and flowcharts appear in the main text, and the programs and notes appear on cards – labelled 7A, 7B, 7C etc. These cards are to be found at the back of the book. Reference to the appropriate card will give information on your particular system.

There are a number of versions of Section 7.1. If you refer to the particular one for your system you will find a copy of the print-out from a typical session at the teleprinter. This section shows you the LOGIN procedure; how to read a paper tape into your work space; how to correct parts of your program; how to SAVE, access and delete programs from your library and the log-out procedure.

121

Program files

If a program is to be used on a number of occasions it should be stored so that it can be loaded into the user's work space quickly and easily.

On some systems a program which is short or is used rarely may be stored on paper tape and loaded through the paper tape reader on the teleprinter. Frequently used programs are most conveniently stored on magnetic disc and can be copied from disc into the user's work space at very high speed. This speed can be hundreds of thousands of characters per second as compared with 10 characters per second for a teleprinter tape reader.

Before a program can be filed on disc it must have a name, usually of no more than six characters. The systems command SAVE causes a copy of the current program in the user's work space to be placed on disc. The command

      KILL – program name
  or UNSAVE – program name

removes the named program from the disc.

To 'call' a program, i.e. to copy it from disc into the work space, the user types

      GET – program name
  or OLD – program name.

A user's own programs are stored on disc under his LOGIN code. These programs can be deleted, added to or modified by him at any time but cannot be accessed by any other user with a different LOGIN code.

Most time-sharing BASIC systems have a public library of standard programs. These can be accessed by any user but, of course, cannot be over-written or modified by any user. These files are known as READ-ONLY files whereas the files in a user's library are known as READ and WRITE files.

Data files

When considering a data file it is necessary to understand the file structure. A file is made up of records, each record usually being capable of holding a number of items of data. For example:

FILE

RECORD 1	ITEM	ITEM	ITEM	ITEM	ITEM . . . etc.
RECORD 2	ITEM	ITEM	ITEM	ITEM	ITEM . . . etc.
RECORD 3					

.
.
.

etc.

In the same way as it was necessary to know the data structure when considering DATA statements as forming a file, the exact location of each item in a data file record must be known.

In Chapter 3, the information on the stock in the warehouse was held in DATA statements. This information can be held in a data file on disc, where it can be subject to interrogation by various programs and, in addition, changed as stock is added or removed from the store. These changes to the file could not have been made by a program when using DATA statements.

The data file could be called STOCK and each record would contain the information on a particular stock item. So we have:

FILE-STOCK

RECORD 1	NUTS	5000	2500	1
RECORD 2	WASHERS	250	200	2
RECORD 3	NAILS	4000	4500	0·5
RECORD 4	HAMMERS	50	45	100
RECORD 5	RIVETS	5000	3000	1
RECORD 6	ENDFILE	0	0	0

Interrogating a file

The original program STKCHK of chapter 3 is shown below with the DATA statements omitted.

```
  20  INPUT I$
  30  IF I$ = "FINISH" THEN 170
  40  READ R$, R1, R2, R3
  50  IF R$ = "ENDFILE" THEN 150
  60  IF I$ ≠ R$ THEN 40
  70  PRINT "ITEM"; R$; "STOCK IS"; R1
* 80  RESTORE
  90  GOTO 20
 150  PRINT "ITEM NOT IN STOCK"
*155  RESTORE
 160  GOTO 20
 170  END
```

If reference is to be made to items in a data file rather than in DATA statements, some changes will be required to this program. Statements which require changing are indicated by a * and the actual changes (as required by the syntax of the files statements in the particular computer system) are shown in the program FILCHK in section 7.2.

Creating a file

The example just considered did not take advantage of the most important features of data files. These are

    1. the ability to refer to any record directly (random access)
    2. the ability to create or change records within a program.

First consider a program which will create the file STOCK. The data for the program could be prepared on paper tape and read by an INPUT statement. This means that at RUN time, a paper tape is placed in the terminal tape reader and the reader is switched on automatically as the INPUT statement is executed.

This may not be possible on all terminals, in which case a series of DATA statements containing the data should be prepared and added to the program (INPUT must then be replaced by READ).

The operations necessary to create a file are shown in the flowchart which follows:

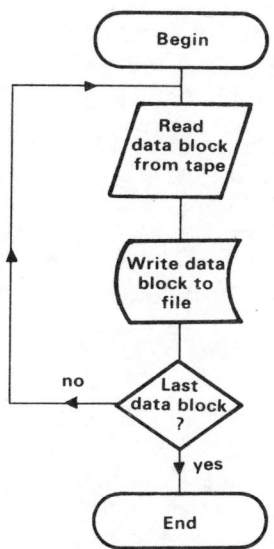

The program (CREATE) to implement this flowchart is given in section 7.3.

While in BASIC it is much quicker to create data files from DATA statements, the program CREATE gives a clearer picture of the creation process.

Printing the Contents of a Data File

A file of the same structure as the file STOCK can be printed out on the teleprinter by a program which is very similar to CREATE. This could be called FILRD and requires changes to the INPUT and PRINT (or WRITE or PUT) statements of CREATE.

A data block ($R\$$, $R1$, $R2$, $R3$) is read from the data file using a READ, GET or INPUT as in statement 40 of FILCHK. The block is then printed using PRINT $R\$$; $R1$; $R2$; $R3$.

Problems 7A

7A.1 Write a program to create a data file containing names. Modify the program REVERS of Ch.3 to print the names in reverse order.

7A.2 Write a program to create a data file containing text and modify the program COUNT 2 of Ch.3 to allow you to analyse the text.

7A.3 The program TROTA of Ch.3 was inelegant as we did not use a facility
for referencing a list of strings. Write a new program to produce the same
output from a list of names on a file.

7A.4 Medical records in a borough include details of births and the dates of
subsequent vaccination schedules. The record for each child could be in
the form:

Name, Date of Birth, Date of 1st Vacc, Date of 2nd, Date of 3rd

e.g. William Smith, 70.10, 71.01, 71.11, 0.

The dates are given in the form 'year.month' and a zero means that
vaccination has not yet been given.

Intervals between the injection should be:

For the 1st – two months after birth
      2nd – ten months after the first
      3rd – six months after the second.

It is always possible that a child has been late with a vaccination.

Write a program which will create the original file.

7A.5 The vaccination file should be interrogated by putting in the current
date and printing out a list of those children due for their 1st, 2nd or
3rd injections. Write a program which performs this interrogation.

7A.6 A firm keeps a file of its employees. A typical record could be

Employee's name; name of department in which employee works;
date of birth; date of entry to the firm; whether paid weekly or
monthly; income tax code number; male or female; married or
single or divorced.

Write a program to create such a file.

The firm wishes to compile lists of employees who come into certain
categories, for example a list of male employees, who are married and
have been with the firm for more than 10 years. Interrogate the file to
obtain lists for a number of such categories.

Keeping a file up to date

The second part of this chapter considers a simple data processing situation based on the earlier stock control problem.

Already established is a data file STOCK containing information on the present stock of items in a warehouse. Since it is possible to change a file, this facility will be used to bring the file STOCK up to date. During the day there may be a number of changes to the stock level as items are withdrawn or supplies received. It is the up-dating of the file STOCK by a list of transactions that is the present concern. The stages in the process are outlined in the following flowchart:

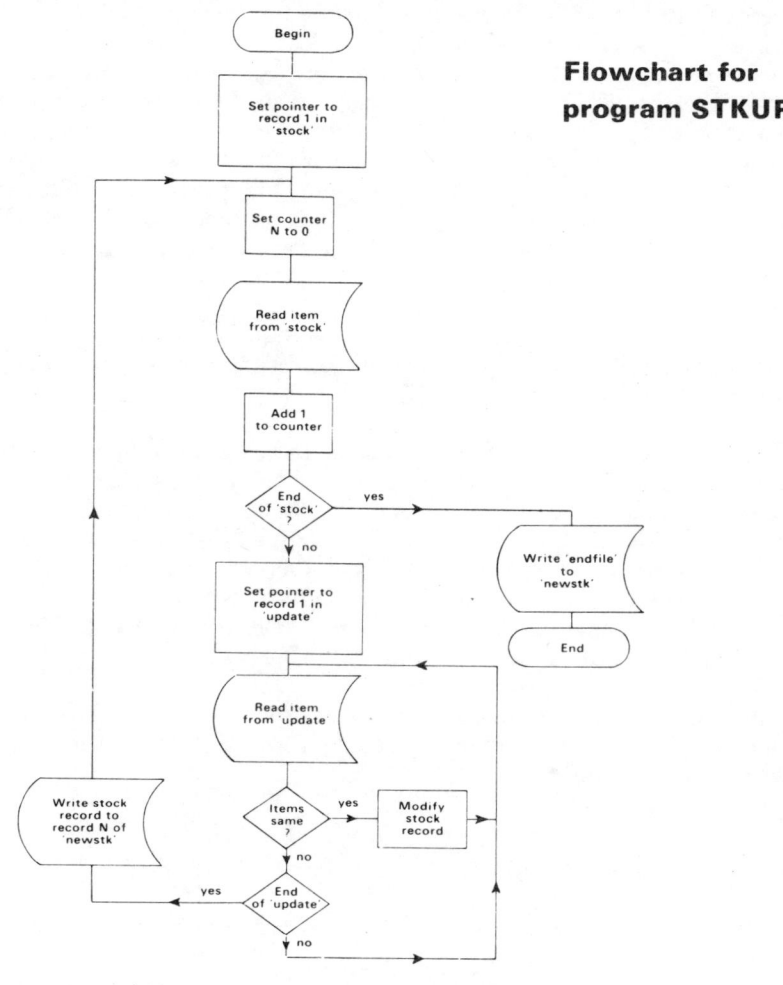

Flowchart for program STKUP

From the flowchart the first operation is seen to be the creation of a transactions file UPDATE. Why is it necessary to create a data file UPDATE instead of directly up-dating the file STOCK from the raw data in DATA statements?

Well, there are a number of reasons for preferring to create a special data file. Firstly, in data processing where many thousands of numbers are processed, it is usual to build-in checks against errors. For example, after performing the stages of the job as shown in the flowchart, a comparison could be made between STOCK and NEWSTK to test that the difference was UPDATE. This sort of procedure is done most efficiently if **all** the information is in the form of a data file. A second equally important reason for creating a trans-actions file is found in the up-dating procedure. The transactions will have taken place, and been recorded, in chronological order. The order of the items in STOCK will be specific, perhaps alphabetical. If STOCK is updated directly from the list of chronological transactions it will be necessary to start at the beginning of STOCK as a search is made for each transaction item. If there are many transactions this means many passes (or at least partial passes) through the stock file. However, if the transactions file is ordered, in the same way as the stock file, before up-dating begins, then a single pass through STOCK will be adequate to update all the items. This is extremely important when there are thousands of items in the files.

In order to keep the examples simple, neither checking or sorting procedures will be included in the solution to the problem. You will be asked to look at these in some of the Problems.7B.

Reference back to the systems flowchart indicates that three operations are to be performed. Three separate programs for these operations will be developed, which may be linked at a later stage. The first program, to create an UPDATE file, is a simple adaption of CREATE and requires little comment. This program, CREUP, puts one transaction in each file record. Each record thus comprises, 'stock item name' and 'change in stock'. The latter will be positive if items are received and negative if items are issued. The program CREUP is shown in section 7.4 together with a run-time print-out.

The second program which creates the file NEWSTK from STOCK and UPDATE, is more complex. A detailed flowchart for the program STKUP could be as shown.

Flowchart for
program STKUP

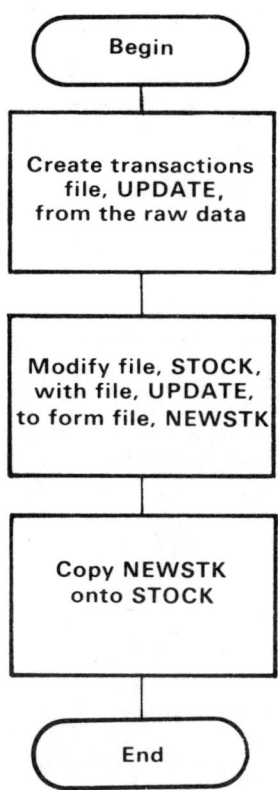

The program STKUP, see Section 7.5, was written on the assumption that the file UPDATE will usually be smaller than STOCK. Thus, each record is taken from STOCK and UPDATE is scanned to see if that item code appears. If it does, and it may occur a number of times, the stock level is modified and once the end of UPDATE is reached, the new stock level is written onto file NEWSTK. If the item does not appear in UPDATE, the record is copied onto NEWSTK unchanged. It would be possible, of course, to write the item straight back onto STOCK and so avoid the formation of a new stock file altogether. This has not been done as it would prevent the possibility of including checks later.

The final program, STKCPY, is perfectly simple. In order to have a file available for interrogation, up-dating, etc. the following day, the file NEWSTK is copied back onto a file named STOCK. This will overwrite the old records with those up-dated by the day's transactions.

Linking programs

Having written and tested each of the programs they can be run linked together as one large integrated program. BASIC allows us to link programs by the use of the CHAIN statement. Programs which are to be linked must be stored on disc and, of course, must have names. A CHAIN statement can be added to any program as the last instruction to be executed and has the form:

CHAIN (program name),

For example, CHAIN FILRD or CHAIN STKCPY.

CHAIN has the effect of three systems commands executed sequentially:

  i) SCRATCH
 ii) GET (or OLD) – program name
iii) RUN.

All time-shared BASIC systems make a certain amount of working core store available to each user. It is possible that the allocated amount is not sufficient for a large program and the data space for variables which it requires. So we have another reason for wishing to make use of the CHAIN facility. Any large program may be segmented and each segment CHAINed to another so that only part of the program is in the core at any one time. But be careful; remember that, as one effect of CHAIN is to clear the present working space (i.e. SCRATCH), then all current data values are lost.

If it is necessary to have a common set of data items for all of the program segments, these must be carefully preserved. This may be done by creating a data file in one segment which is read by a subsequent segment so allowing the values of required variables to be saved. The flowchart for such a series of segments could be drawn as follows:

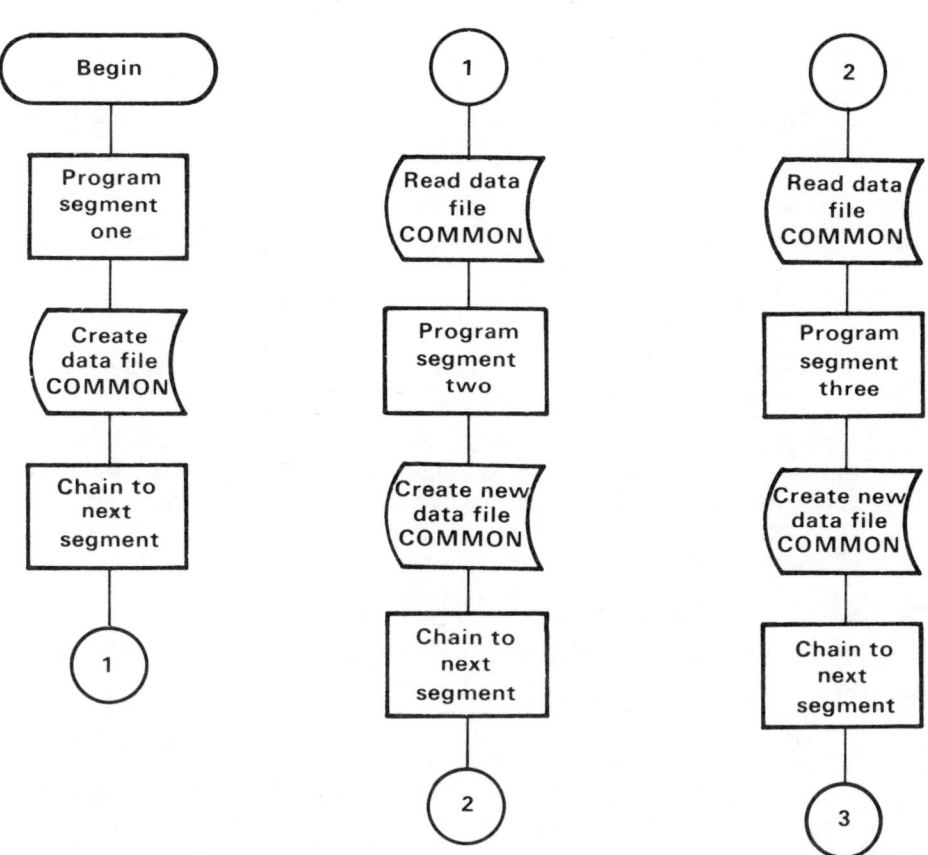

Problems 7B

7B.1   Numeric swop sorting was explained in Chapter 6 and a suggestion for alphanumeric string comparison given in problems 3C. Given the ability to store a list of strings in a data file, the swop-sorting principle can be used to order a list of strings.

Write a program to sort a list of names using one or more data files.

7B.2   Extend 7B.1 to allow sorting of whole records on a key. For example, sort files STOCK and UPDATE into alphabetic order of the item name. Modify the program STKUP to take advantage of the ordered files and reduce the number of data manipulations required.

7B.3   The problem of errors recurring in data processing file manipulation was mentioned in the chapter. Modify the program STKUP to include a check that the up-dating process took place correctly.

7B.4   A bank's records can be taken to be of the form –

Customer's name, present balance at the bank (positive or negative!) overdraft limit, limit on any particular transaction.

Input a typical set of transactions for a day's work, and use them to bring the bank's records up to date. Warnings should be printed out if transaction limits or overdraft limits have been exceeded. A warning must also be printed out if the day's transactions include any names which do not appear in the bank's records.

7B.5   Write a program which creates a file on the vaccinations given to children so that the medical records file of problem 7A.4 can be up-dated.

7B.6   An electricity board keeps a record of the meter readings of its consumers on a computer file. Each quarter a new file is created which consists of all the new readings. This new file is compared with the old one and consumers' accounts for the previous quarter are calculated. Write programs which creates the new file and then produce the accounts.

Chapter 8

Matrices

Entering and printing matrices

An interesting feature of many versions of BASIC is a set of special statements for handling matrices. In this chapter we shall give only a brief summary of the statements and shall assume that the reader has already met the necessary mathematics of matrices.

Before matrices can be used in a program they must be dimensioned, to reserve storage space, as was mentioned in Chapter 4. Once a matrix has been dimensioned the values of its elements can be read in from a data statement and then the array can be printed out. In the program below line 10 defines A and B as 2 by 2 matrices and line 20 reads the values of the elements of A and B from the data statement 40. The elements are read in row order, that is to say $A(1, 1)$, $A(1, 2)$, $A(2, 1)$, $A(2, 2)$ and similarly for B. Statement 30 displays the matrices as seen in the print-out. Notice that B is not displayed on the same line as A as would be the case in a simple PRINT A, B statement.

```
10  DIM A(2,2),B(2,2)
20  MAT READ A,B
30  MAT PRINT A,B
40  DATA 1,2,3,4,5,6,7,8
50  END

RUN


MADIS1     12:18   G265 B 23/12/71

 1               2

 3               4


 5               6

 7               8
```

133

Matrix arithmetic

Now that the elements of A and B have values, the matrices can be combined in the usual ways.

MAT $C = A + B$ adds matrices A and B and stores the result in C. The dimensions of A, B and C must be conformable – an error message is usually received if this is not the case, and execution is stopped. MAT $C = A - B$ and MAT $C = A*B$ operate similarly. Note that the matrix C must have been dimensioned before it is used in any of these statements, and only one matrix operation can be performed in each statement. The accompanying program and print-out illustrate the use of these statements.

```
                                          MAD1S2      12:20     G265 B 23/12/71

                                          MATRIX A
                                          1                   2

                                          3                   4
10 DIM A(2,2),B(2,2),C(2,2)
20 MAT READ A,B
30 PRINT "MATRIX A"                        MATRIX B
40 MAT PRINT A                             5                   6
50 PRINT "MATRIX B"
60 MAT PRINT B                             7                   8
70 MAT C=A+B
80 PRINT "A+B"
90 MAT PRINT C                             A+B
100 MAT C=A-B                              6                   8
110 PRINT "A-B"
120 MAT PRINT C                            10                  12
130 MAT C=A*B
140 PRINT "A X B"
150 MAT PRINT C                            A-B
160 DATA 1,2,3,4,5,6,7,8                   -4                  -4
170 END
                                           -4                  -4


                                           A X B
                                           19                  22

                                           43                  50
```

It is possible to have statements of the form

MAT $A = A + B$ and even MAT $A = A - A$

but the same matrix is not allowed to appear on both sides of the equals sign when multiplication is used. It is also possible to refer to particular elements of a matrix during a program. For instance, after the matrix

$$\begin{pmatrix} 1 & 2 & 3 \\ 4 & 5 & 6 \end{pmatrix}$$

has been read by a program from a data statement, the same program can refer to the subscripted variables $A(1, 1)$ or $A(2, 3)$ etc. and use these in statements in the program. This is done in the program MATEL, below, in order to alter certain elements in the matrix.

```
10  DIM A(2,3)
20  MAT READ A
30  MAT PRINT A
40  LET A(1,1)=A(1,1)*4
50  LET A(1,3)=0
60  LET A(2,1)=A(2,2)+A(2,3)
70  MAT PRINT A
80  DATA 1,2,3,4,5,6
90  END

RUN


MATEL        12:26     G265 B 23/12/71

  1              2               3

  4              5               6


  4              2               0

 11              5               6
```

Other useful statements are:

MAT B = INV (A) which inverts matrix A and stores the result in B

MAT B = TRN (A) which transposes matrix A and stores the
result in B

MAT B = $(K)*A$ which multiplies matrix A by K, where K may
be either a number or an expression.

You should note that statements

MAT A = INV (A) and MAT A = TRN (A)

are not allowed.

The use of these statements should be fairly obvious and perhaps it should
again be said that great care must be taken with the dimensions of the matrices
involved. Some versions of BASIC will produce an error message if an attempt
is made to invert a singular matrix.

There are three further statements which can be used:

MAT A = CON   which makes each element of the matrix A
equal to 1

MAT A = ZER   which makes each element of matrix A
equal to 0

MAT A = IDN   which makes the elements of the leading
diagonal of matrix a equal to 1, and all the
other elements equal to 0. A must be a square
matrix.

Redimensioning matrices

Greater flexibility in a program can be obtained by making use of slightly extended forms of some of the statements mentioned. These extended forms dimension the matrix at the same time as performing the function already described. This does not do away with the need for a DIM statement covering every matrix to be used in the program. The DIM statement specifies the *maximum* amount of storage that will be reserved for each matrix.

The four statements are:

$$\text{MAT READ } A \ (P, Q)$$
$$\text{MAT } A = \text{ZER } (P, Q)$$
$$\text{MAT } A = \text{CON } (P, Q)$$
$$\text{MAT } A = \text{IDN } (P, P)$$

the first three specifying A as having P rows and Q columns, and the fourth specifying A as being square with P rows and columns. Using these statements it is possible to re-dimension a matrix while the program is running. The change may be to either a larger or a smaller matrix, provided that the dimensions as given in the DIM statement are not exceeded. The program MATEX demonstrates the use of these statements.

Program 'MATEX'

```
 10 DIM A(6,6),B(6,6),C(6,6),D(6,6),E(6,6)
 20 MAT READ A(3,3),B(3,3)
 30 MAT C=ZER(3,3)
 40 MAT C=A+B
 50 PRINT "MATRIX A"
 60 MAT PRINT A
 70 PRINT "MATRIX B"
 80 MAT PRINT B
 90 PRINT "A+B"
100 MAT PRINT C
110 READ P,Q
120 MAT D=CON(P,Q)
130 MAT E=IDN(P,P)
140 MAT D=(4)*D
150 PRINT "4 X MATRIX CON"
160 MAT PRINT D
170 MAT E=(10)*E
180 PRINT "10 X MATRIX IDN"
190 MAT PRINT E
200 DATA 1,2,-2,4,0,3,1,2,0,4,6,-3,1,2,1,-2,-3,1,4,5
210 END
```

```
RUN


MATEX      12:32    G265 B 23/12/71
MATRIX A
  1                2                -2

  4                0                 3

  1                2                 0


MATRIX B
  4                6                -3

  1                2                 1

 -2               -3                 1


A+B
  5                8                -5

  5                2                 4

 -1               -1                 1


4 X MATRIX CON
  4                4                4             4             4

  4                4                4             4             4

  4                4                4             4             4

  4                4                4             4             4


10 X MATRIX IDN
 10                0                0             0

  0               10                0             0

  0                0               10             0

  0                0                0            10
```

Problems 8

8.1   Solve the equations $2x + 3y = 21$
                              $5x - 2y = 5$

using a matrix method. Can you incorporate a check on the answers produced?

8.2   Extend your method for 8.1 to deal with any simultaneous equations in two unknowns. Remember to check the value of the determinant!

8.3   Write a program which will accept as input the coordinates of a point and prints the coordinates of the point under the transformation

$$\begin{pmatrix} 1 & 0 \\ 2 & 1 \end{pmatrix}$$

Extend your program to accept as input the matrix of the required transformation and then to accept the coordinates and calculate the image as before.

8.4   Write a program with which you can investigate powers of matrices (that is $A^2 = A \times A$, $A^3 = A \times A \times A$ etc). The program should accept as input the matrix and the required power.

8.5   Use your program for 8.4 to investigate powers of probability matrices, that is matrices in which the sum of the elements of each separate row is equal to 1.

8.6   Chemistry sets in a toy-shop come in four different sizes, Sets A, B, C and D whose prices are £0·75, £1·75, £2·50 and £3·75. A certain shop, say shop number 1, orders 10 of type A, 20 of type B, 15 of type C and 5 of type D. Write a program using matrices, which will accept as input the shop's order and calculates the cost of that order. Extend your program to deal with a number of shops, the cost for each shop and the total cost.

8.7   In a general matrix routine it may be necessary to handle matrices of various dimensions. One way is to start the program

> 10 INPUT P, Q
> 20 MAT $A = $ ZER(P, Q)

and then to input elements with nested FOR loops. Write a program to accept, firstly the size of a matrix and then the elements of the matrix. The program should then print out the matrix.

8.8   One way to find the square root of a number by an iterative process is as follows. To find the square root of 7, first make a guess at the square root (say 2·5) and write this as a fraction but using a 2 by 1 matrix e.g.

$$\begin{pmatrix} 5 \\ 2 \end{pmatrix}$$

This 'guess' matrix is then multiplied by the matrix

$$\begin{pmatrix} 1 & 7 \\ 1 & 1 \end{pmatrix}$$

and the result is a new estimate for the required square root. The multiplication by

$$\begin{pmatrix} 1 & 7 \\ 1 & 1 \end{pmatrix}$$

is then continued until an answer with the required accuracy is obtained. To find the square root of n the multiplying matrix is

$$\begin{pmatrix} 1 & n \\ 1 & 1 \end{pmatrix}$$

Write a program to investigate this method of finding square roots.

Chapter 9

A Problem Miscellany

The exercises within this book have been designed partly to familiarise the reader with the features of the BASIC language and partly to give practice in using these features to extend programming techniques. There are two important considerations which limit the value of problems of this kind:

in a practical problem, the programmer is given no guidance on the method to be used, and

a practical problem is not an exercise. The programming is part of a problem area which may involve analysis of a situation and design of a framework or system within which the problem must be tackled – systems analysis and design, in fact. Indeed, part of the job may be to define the problem to be programmed.

The following problems attempt to ilustrate these two aspects of practical programming. The reader should not expect well defined problems and rarely is there any indication of the features of BASIC which should be used. The sections should be regarded as problem areas within which many investigations can be made, some of these involving only simple programs.

Clearly these problems cannot be graded, nor can they be classified.

9.1 Banking procedures and real time data entry

As an illustration of this situation allocate code numbers or passwords to each of a number of bank clerks. These, and only these clerks may enter data to a bank's accounts. Programs should be written to allow some of the following to appear during a computer run:

Accounts may be set up or cancelled, each account having an account number.

If an account is set up for a clerk, he may not have access to that account.

Details of a deposit or withdrawal may be entered to an account.

Money may be transferred between accounts.

Each account contains an overdraft 'barrier', which will stop a withdrawal if the resulting debit balance is below a certain level. Bank charges are included.

The current state of an account may be printed – a clerk may ask for the state of his own account.

Further procedures should be added as appropriate.

9.2 Repetition testing

Program COUNT1 of chapter 3 counted the repetitions of a specific word in a sentence. The more general problem of testing for repetition within a set of items has many applications which include:

Text analysis

Student records – to ensure that two or more people having the same name are not confused.

Holiday booking – within an organisation it may be necessary to ensure that not too many employees are on holiday at the same time.

Write a program to enter three numbers and to test whether 1, 2 or all 3 are equal.

Extend the ideas written into your program for three numbers to cope with a general list of numbers or strings, printing all repetitions with their corresponding frequencies. A further extension would be to have a list of two or more items – say christian name, surname and age in years – and obtain a print-out of people with the same age or people of the same christian name.

9.3 In how many different ways . . . ?   (1)

Input a sum of money (less than £5) and print out the number and type of coins and notes needed to make up that sum. You may care to extend the program to answer the question – 'In how many different ways can a sum of (say) £1·24 be made up?'. Of more practical significance is the following situation:

> A small firm pays its 20 employees in cash each week. It is essential that the cashier collects change from the bank so that he can make up the pay packets beforehand. Write a program which demands the pay for each employee and provides, at the end, a list of the number and type of coins and notes needed by the cashier.

9.4 In how many different ways . . . ?   (2)

Games or competitions which involve the scoring of points sometimes raise the problem of the number of ways in which a particular target may be reached. One of the most common situations of this kind occurs in the game of darts, where one may ask the question – 'in how many different ways is it possible to score a given total on a dartboard, using up to three darts?'. Write a program to investigate this problem.

9.5 Data checking

It is important that data used in any calculation should be reliable, but especially so in computer calculations and data processing where vast amounts of data are used. Programs can include checks on the data and methods of data vetting are many and varied.

It may be necessary, where the order of the data is predetermined, for the program to check that order. Write a program to enter a list of numbers and to print out any which are not in numerically ascending order. Alternatively you could use words and alphabetic order.

Further examples of checking methods are the inclusion of bounds to ensure that the data lies within sensible limits and the introduction of extraneous information which can be calculated from the data and then used for cross checking. This latter method may be seen in the use of check digits.

There are many ways of forming a check digit, of which the following is probably the most simple:

taking the number 5841, add the digits $5+8+4+1$ to obtain 18 and use the final digit of the result, 8, as the check digit. The check digit is tagged on to the end of the original number, giving 58418. If the number were miscopied as 88418 the check digit would no longer tally with the number.

Write a program to check the check digit.

Note that this method of forming a check digit does not guard against the number being miscopied as 85418. Another method must be used.

9.6 Inside or outside?

Write a program to enter a list of numbers and count how many of them are above a certain level (also to be entered). How many of them lie above this level but below another (higher) level?

The simple procedures described above may be applied to a number of situations and examples have already been suggested in problems 9.1 and 9.5. Other examples of the use of critical boundaries may be found in linear programming and quality control. One other application follows:

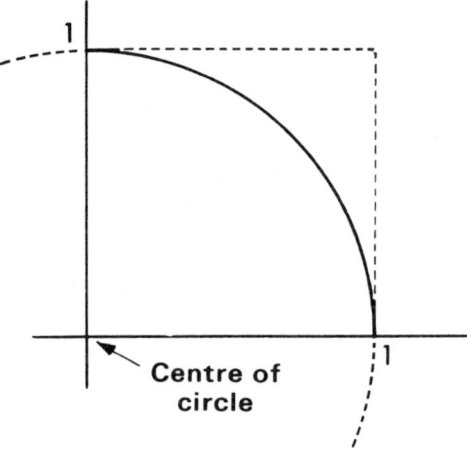

Centre of circle

Using the RND function, a pair of random numbers may be used to fix the position of a point in a unit square. Write a program which tests whether the point lies inside the quarter circle which has its centre at a corner of the square, as shown. The program should then repeat this for a large number of points, keeping a count of those lying inside the circle. Of the total points, the fraction lying inside the circle should approximate to the area of the quarter circle and hence an estimate of π may be obtained.

This method of finding areas, known as a Monte Carlo method, may be compared with the methods suggested in Chapter 5.

9.7 Sports records

Input the race numbers of the runners in a cross-country race in the order in which they finish. Print-out the results of the race, both for the individual and the team positions.

The computer analysis and presentation of sports results has been seen at a number of major events since the mid 1960's. Essentially the problem is one of real-time data entry but programming ideas may be investigated even where a terminal is not available. To perform an investigation, consider an athletics match in which there are four teams:

FOXES; WOLVES; BADGERS; FERRETS.

Each competitor has a number and is a member of team – although the teams may not all have the same number of members. After each event, the data received is:

Name of event
Numbers of first three competitors.

Printout should give the event, the names and teams of the first three competitors and the current team scores.

Elaborations on this could include variable scoring systems for different events and the introduction of bonus points for 'record breaking'.

9.8 The longest ladder

What is the length of the longest ladder that can be carried horizontally round a right-angled corner in a corridor 8′ wide?

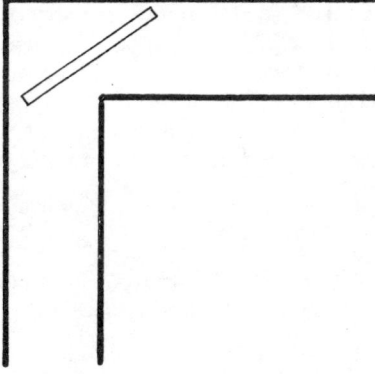

Although this may be tackled analytically without a computer, an iterative approach would seem reasonable. This is particularly the case if the geometry gets more difficult – for example if the width of the corridor changes and the angle is not a right angle.

One practical problem which required such an iterative approach was in connection with shell-plating on the sides of ships. These plates are not quite rectangles and this raises a question of optimisation: 'What is the smallest rectangle from which it is possible to cut a given quadrilateral?'.

9.9 Random numbers

There are many ways of generating random numbers in a computer. The sequences obtained are always pseudo random and the question of their suitability arises. This is particularly true when many trials are required in a simulation or in a process such as that of question 9.6. An investigation can be made of various methods of generation and the results from these can be compared with the RND function available. It may be that some procedures will involve less machine time, a fact which may be established by containing the procedure within a loop and repeating the loop a large number of times. Tests which may be made on whether the numbers generated behave like random numbers include:

> If the range of numbers is split into equal divisions, the frequencies with which numbers from a large set fall within these divisions should be equal.

> The average of a large set of numbers should be the middle value of the range.

> A zero correlation co-efficient should be obtained between adjacent numbers.

9.10 Number bases

At one time it was felt that a mastery of binary arithmetic was necessary for an understanding of the computer. Consequently practice in binary–denary and denary–binary conversion was evident in many courses. It is now recognised that what is more important is an appreciation of variety in numbering systems. Various computer procedures may be written to explore relationships between numbering systems and a few are suggested:

9.10.1 Write a program which converts a decimal number to its binary equivalent.

9.10.2 Write a program which converts a decimal number to its binary coded decimal equivalent.

9.10.3 Write a program which converts a number in Base M to its equivalent in Base N. The program should initially restrict M and N to be both below ten. It may then be extended.

9.10.4 Write a program which will add together two numbers in Base M.
This should be done without conversion to binary.

9.11 Guessing games

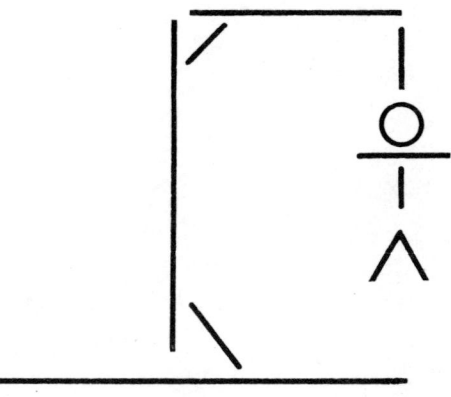

In the familiar game of 'hangman'
a word is chosen by one player and
his opponent has to guess the
word by choosing letters. At each
stage the opponent is shown a
series of blanks and correctly
chosen letters. E.g., if the word is
'HANGMAN' and he has guessed
M and A he would be shown
–A––M––. As an alternative to a
letter, he may guess at the whole
word. For each wrong guess (letter
or word), one part of the gallows
drawing is made. After the tenth,
the drawing is complete and the
opponent has lost.

In writing a computer program for this game, a word (entered in a DATA
statement) is to be guessed by a player at the terminal. The player may enter a
guessed letter or word, the computer printing the successful guesses and,
possibly, a picture of the part complete gallows.

Card Supplements
to Chapter 7

Card
Number System

7A	Burroughs 700 Series
7B	Computer Technology-Modular 1
7C	Digital Equipment Corporation-System 10
7D	Hewlett Packard 2000 Series
7E	Honeywell Time Sharing
7F	IBM Call/360
7G	ICL-1900
7H	ICL-System 4
7I	Xerox Data Systems-Sigma 5-Sigma 9

Each supplement contains six sections

7·1	Filed program manipulation
7·2	Program FILCHK
7·3	Program CREATE
7·4	Program CREUP
7·5	Program STKUP
7·6	Program STKCPY

Section 7A: Burroughs 700 Series

7·1   Filed program manipulation

Input via the teleprinter keyboard is underlined. Each line of input is terminated by keying 'CTRL' and 'C' together. 'CTRL' and 'H' keyed together delete the previous character on the line and may be used repeatedly. The whole of the current line may be deleted by the 'RUBOUT' key. The system responds with 'DEL'.

```
GOOD AFTERNOON, B-6700 DATACOM ANSWERING
ENTER USERCODE, PLEASE
ROGERS
ENTER PASSWORD, PLEASE
███████████████████                      —Overprinting obscures password.
ENTER RECOVERY NUMBER TO RECOVER WORKFILE, ELSE SEND ETX.
—                                         —Control C is keyed.
TIME=17:46 ON 09/08/72
MCS LEVEL = II.2.00
YOUR RECOVERY NUMBER IS 1
CONTINUE                                   Work file is set up. BASIC record
CREATE SUMS BASIC                         —layout to be used (not e.g. FORTRAN
#                                          or data).
SEQ 10+10                                 —The machine is to produce sequence
10  READ A,B,C,D,E,                        nos.
20  PRINT A,;B;C;D;E                       —Control H used to delete comma.
30  PRINT A+B;B+C;C+D;D+E;E+A
40  DETA 10,20,25,12,16
50
#                                         —Control C is keyed.
FILES
#                                         —"What files are on backing store?"
SAVE                                       There are no files currently stored.
END SAVE (0.1 SEC.)                       —Copy work file to backing store.
COMPILE
                                          —Compile the work file.
FILE(SYSTEM/BASIC,ERRORFILE) OPEN ------
ERR-READ LIST ELEMENT MUST BE ARITHMETIC OR STRING VARIABLE      AT #0010
ERR-LEFT PAREN OR ASSIGNMENT OPERATOR EXPECTED                   AT #0040
END SUMS COMPILE ERRORS (0.4 SEC.)
FILE(SYSTEM/BASIC,ERRORFILE) CLOSED ----
10READ A,B,C,D,E                          —Correction of errors detected on
40DATA 10,20,25,12,16                      compilation.
FILES
SUMS (S)                                  —This is the uncorrected source
#                                          program.
COMPILE
#
END SUMS COMPILE (0.5 SEC.)               —No errors now.
SAVE
END SAVE (0.3 SEC.)                       —Correct source and object programs
FILES                                      are filed.
SUMS (S&O)
#
```

151

```
EXECUTE(BCARD,BLINE)
#
```
—*Run the program equating the input file B CARD and the output file B LINE to the remote device.*

```
FILE(ROGERS/SUMS/OBJECT,BLINE) OPEN ----
  10      20     25     12     16
  30      45     37     28     26
SUMS EOJ (0.1 SEC.)
FILE(ROGERS/SUMS/OBJECT,BLINE) CLOSED --
WHATS
WORK FILE SUMS TYPE BASIC
REMOVE
#
WHATS
NO WORK FILE
WHATS SUMS
FILE SUMS TYPE BASIC 08/09/72 4 RECORDS
E SUMS(BLINE)
#
```
—*A blank name implies the work file.*

—*Clear work file.*

—*EXECUTE may be abbreviated to E.*

```
FILE(ROGERS/SUMS/OBJECT,BLINE) OPEN ----
  10      20.    25     12     16
  30      45     37     28     26
SUMS EOJ (0.1 SEC.)
FILE(ROGERS/SUMS/OBJECT,BLINE) CLOSED --
REMOVE SUMS
#
FILES
#
BYDEL
LOAD SUMS
              * ERR NO FILE
BYE
ON-LINE     8 MIN
PROC. TIME  2 SEC
I/O TIME    8 SEC
GOODBYE
```
—*Delete SUMS from file.*

—*'DEL' was in response to 'RUBOUT'.*

7·2 Program FILCHK

Based on the earlier program STKCHK.

```
LIST FILCHK
FILE FILCHK TYPE BASIC 05/09/72 13 RECORDS
10 FILES STOCK = "ROGERS/STOCK/SOURCE"
20 INPUT I$
30 IF I$ = "FINISH" THEN 130
40 INPUT #1,R$,R1,R2,R3
50 IF R$ = "ENDFILE" THEN 100
60 IF I$ <> R$ THEN 40
70 PRINT "ITEM";R$;"STOCK IS";R1
80 RESTORE #1
90 GOTO 20
100 PRINT "ITEM NOT IN STOCK"
110 RESTORE #1
120 GOTO 20
130 END
```

Statement 10	Specifies the data file to be used.
Statement 40	Is interpreted as: read four items of data from the first file mentioned in the program. The items are a string and three numerics to be called *R$*, *R1*, *R2*, *R3*.

Statements 80 and 110   Both have a similar action to the use of RESTORE with DATA statements. RESTORE #1 moves the pointer for file 1 back to the first item in the file.

7·3   Program CREATE

```
LIST CREATE
FILE CREATE TYPE BASIC 05/09/72 5 RECORDS
10 FILES STOCK = "ROGERS/STOCK/SOURCE"
20 INPUT R$,R1,R2,R3
30 PRINT #1,R$,R1,R2,R3
40 IF R$ <> "ENDFILE" THEN 20
50 END
END LIST (0.1 SEC.)
```

Note the use of the PRINT statement, even though File 1 is a disc file. No special action is required to create the file. If one of the same name is already present, it will have its contents over-written by the new records.

The text in quotes in line 10 is the external name of the file. It follows the naming conventions of 'CANDE'* so that the results can be accessed from the terminal.

Files are found on disc using their external names but handled in programs using their internal names or numbers.

```
EXECUTE CREATE(BLINE,BCARD)
#
FILE(ROGERS/CREATE/OBJECT,BLINE) OPEN ----
FILE(ROGERS/CREATE/OBJECT,BCARD) OPEN ----
?"NUTS",500,2500,1
?"WASHERS",250,200,2
?"NAILS",4000,4500,0.5
?"HAMMERS",50,45,100
?"RIVETS",5000,3000,1
?"ENDFILE",0,0,0
FILE(ROGERS/CREATE/OBJECT,BCARD) CLOSED --
FILE(ROGERS/CREATE/OBJECT,BLINE) CLOSED --
CREATE EOJ (0.3 SEC.)
```

*Languages other than BASIC may be handled under this 'CANDE' (command and edit) system. For further details see the CANDE and BASIC manuals.

7·4   Program CREUP

```
LIST CREUP
FILE CREUP TYPE BASIC 05/09/72 5 RECORDS
10 FILES UPDATE = "ROGERS/UPDATE/SOURCE"
20 INPUT R$,R1
30 PRINT #1,R$,R1
40 IF R$ <> "ENDUP" THEN 20
50 END
END LIST (0.1 SEC.)
```

EXECUTE is again abbreviated to E in the next
line of printout.

```
E CREUP(BCARD,BLINE)
#
FILE (ROGERS/CREUP/OBJECT,BLINE) OPEN ----
FILE (ROGERS/CREUP/OBJECT,BCARD) OPEN ----
?"NAILS",-200
?"HAMMERS",-5
?"NUTS",-200
?"NAILS",-150
?"ENDUP",0
CREUP EOJ (0.2 SEC.)
FILE(ROGERS/CREUP/OBJECT,BCARD) CLOSED --
FILE(ROGERS/CREUP/OBJECT,BLINE) CLOSED --
```

A printout of the contents of the file STOCK may
now be obtained using the CANDE command
PRINT.

```
PRINT STOCK
1000 "NUTS", 5000, 2500, 1,
1010 "WASHERS", 250, 200, 2,
1020 "NAILS", 4000, 4500, 0.5,
1030 "HAMMERS", 50, 45, 100,
1040 "RIVETS", 5000, 3000, 1,
1050 "ENDFILE", 0, 0, 0,
#
```

7·5   Program STKUP

```
PRINT STKUP
10 FILES STOCK = "ROGERS/STOCK/SOURCE"
20 FILES UPDATE = "ROGERS/UPDATE/SOURCE"
30 FILES NEWSTK = "ROGERS/NEWSTK/SOURCE"
40 INPUT #1,R$,R1,R2,R3
50 IF R$ = "ENDFILE" THEN 140
60 INPUT #2,S$,S1
70 IF R$ = S$ THEN 120
80 IF S$ <> "ENDUP" THEN 60
90 RESTORE #2
100 PRINT #3,R$,R1,R2,R3
110 GOTO 40
120 LET R1=R1+S1
130 GOTO 60
140 PRINT #3,"ENDFILE",0,0,0
150 END
#
```

The program STKUP uses the UPDATE file to
update the file STOCK to a new file NEWSTK.
The contents of NEWSTK are printed using the
CANDE command PRINT.

```
PRINT NEWSTK
1000 "NUTS", 4800, 2500, 1,
1010 "WASHERS", 250, 200, 2,
1020 "NAILS", 3650, 4500, 0.5,
1030 "HAMMERS", 45, 45, 100,
1040 "RIVETS", 5000, 3000, 1,
1050 "ENDFILE", 0, 0, 0,
```

7·6   Program STKCPY

This program completes the update cycle by
overwriting the old stock file with a new one.

```
PRINT STKCPY
10 FILES NEWSTK = "ROGERS/NEWSTK/SOURCE"
11 FILES STOCK = "ROGERS/STOCK/SOURCE"
20 INPUT #1,R$,R1,R2,R3
30 PRINT #2,R$,R1,R2,R3
40 IF R$ <> "ENDFILE" THEN 20
50 END
#
```

Section 7B: Computer Technology— Modular One

7·1 Filed program manipulation

Input via the teleprinter keyboard is underlined.

```
SERVICE HRS TODAY ARE FROM 0930 TO 2130 HRS.
LONDON  27/01/72
CONNECTED AT 16·46 ON CHANNEL  0
USER NUMBER:HEU212
ILLEGAL ACCESS

USER NUMBER:HEU212
PROJECT ID:ARS

LANGUAGE:BASIC

*10 READ A,B,C,D,E,
*20 PRINT A;B;C;D;E
*30 PRINT A+B;B+C;C+D;E+B\A
*40 DETA 10,20,25,12,16
*RUN

RUN ERROR    30 IN LINE    10
RUN ERROR     3 IN LINE    40
RUN ERROR    58 IN LINE    30

COMPILATION COMPLETE

RAN 1 SECONDS
*10 READ A,B,C,D,E
*40 DATA 10,20,25,12·\,16
*50 END
*RUN


 10  20  25  12  16
 30  45  37  26

COMPLETED
RAN 1 SECONDS
*STORE SUMS
*LIST

USER  HEU212  ARS  27/01/72
  10 READ A,B,C,D,E
  20 PRINT A;B;C;D;E
  30 PRINT A+B;B+C;C+D;E+A
  40 DATA 10,20,25,12,16
  50 END
```

—Introductory messages.

—A password follows the user number. The printing of this is suppressed.

—User reference for internal accounting.

—The \ is used to delete the previous character.

—Errors detected during compilation.

—Correction of errors.

—Successful run.

—Program named and filed in a single command.

157

```
*DELETEALL                                    —Clear the work space.
*LIST


USER  HEU212  ARS  27/01/72              ⎤—There is no current program to be
                                         ⎦ listed.
NO WORK FILE
*LOAD SUMS                                    —Load file 'SUMS' into work space.
*RUN

   10   20   25   12   16
   30   45   37   26

COMPLETED
RAN 1 SECONDS
*INDEX                                        —Request  for  catalogue  of  filed
                                               programs.

USER  HEU212  27/01/72

   NAME      I.D.  LENGTH  DATE    LANGUAGE
RL1          RL      1   26/ 1/72  BASIC
SUMS         ARS     1   27/ 1/72  BASIC
*ERASE SUMS                                   —Remove 'SUMS' from file.

*LOAD SUMS                                    —'SUMS' has been removed from file.

FILE NOT STORED
*LOGOUT

USER  HEU212  ARS  27/01/72
TIME ON 16.46 TIME OFF 16.56
CONNECTED TIME  10 MINUTES
COMPUTE TIME  4 SECONDS

DISCONNECTED
              X
```

7·2 Program FILCHK

Based on the earlier program STKCHK.

```
  5   FILES STOCK
 10   DIM R$(10),  I$(10)
 20   INPUT I$
 30   IF I$=''FINISH'' THEN 170
 40   READ % 1;R$,R1,R2,R3
 50   IF R$=''ENDFILE'' THEN 160
 60   IF R$ <> I$ THEN 40
 70   PRINT ''ITEM '';R$;'' STOCK IS '';R1
 80   READ % 1,1
 90   GOTO 20
150   PRINT ''ITEM NOT IN STOCK''
155   READ % 1,1
160   GOTO 20
170   END
```

Statement 5   Specifies the data files to be used in the program.

Statement 40   Is interpreted as: read four items of data from the first named file in the FILES list. The items are a string and three numerics to be called *R\$*, *R1*, *R2*, *R3*.

Statements 80 and 155   Both have a similar action to RESTORE. When reading data from a file sequentially, a pointer keeps check on which item is to be read next.

7·3   Program CREATE

```
LIST

USER  HEU212  RL  03/02/72
   10 FILES STOCK
   20 DIM R$(10)
   30 LET N=1
   40 INPUT R$,R1,R2,R3
   50 PRINT %1,N;R$,R1,R2,R3
   60 LET N=N+1
   70 IF R$<>"ENDFILE" THEN 40
   80 END
```

PRINT %1, N; (variable names) allows a particular record to be referenced. If   , N   is omitted the items would be automatically stored sequentially.

In the RUN which follows it will be noted that the familiar '?' in response to INPUT is replaced by ':'. After two items have been written onto file a systems message confirms that a file, named by the program, in this case STOCK, is being created. If the data file produced is to be saved, the reply to STORE FILES? is YES.

```
*RUN

   :"NUTS",5000,2500,1
   :"WASHERS",250,200,1

FILE   STOCK CREATED
   :"NAILS",4000,4500,0.5
   :"HAMMERS",50,45,100
   :R\"RIVETS",5000,3000,1
   :"ENDFILE",0,0,0

COMPLETED
STORE FILES?  :YES
STORED

RAN  1 SECONDS
   *
```

7·4   Program CREUP

```
 DELETEALL
*LOAD CREUP
*LIST


 .
USER  HEU212  RL  03/02/72
   10 FILES UPDATE
   20 DIM R$(10)
   30 LET N=1
   40 INPUT R$,R1
   50 PRINT %1,N;R$,R1
   60 LET N=N+1
   70 IF R$<> "ENDUP" THEN 40
   80 END
*RUN


 :"NAILS",-200
 :"HAMMERS",-5

FILE   UPDATE CREATED
 :"NUTS",-200
 :"NAILS",-150
 :"ENDUP,0

RUN ERROR    73 IN LINE    40

RE-INPUT FROM ITEM      1
 :"ENDUP",0

COMPLETED
STORE FILES? :YES
STORED
```

7·5   Program STKUP

```
 DELETE ALL
*LOAD STKUP
*LIST


USER  HEU212  RL  03/02/72
   10 FILES STOCK,UPDATE,NEWSTK
   20 READ %1,1
   30 LET N=0
   40 DIM R$(10),S$(10)
   45 LET N=N+1
   50 READ %1;R$,R1,R2,R3
   60 IF R$="ENDFILE" THEN 160
   70 READ %2,1
   80 READ %2;S$,S1
   90 IF R$<>S$ THEN 120
  100 LET R1=R1+S1
  110 GOTO 80
  120 IF S$="ENDUP" THEN 140
  130 GOTO 80
  140 PRINT %3,N;R$,R1,R2,R3
  150 GOTO 45
  160 PRINT %3,N;"ENDFILE",0,0,0
  165 PRINT
  170 PRINT "END OF UPDATE"
  200 END
*
```

```
 DELETE ALL
*LOAD FILRD
*RUN


FILE   STOCK   LOADED
NUTS 5000   2500   1
WASHERS 250   200   1
NAILS 4000    4500   .5
HAMMERS 50   45   100
RIVETS 5000   3000   1
ENDFILE 0   0   0

COMPLETED
RAN 1 SECONDS
*DELETE ALL
*LOAD STKUP
*RUN


FILE   STOCK   LOADED

FILE   UPDATE   LOADED

FILE   NEWSTK CREATED

END OF UPDATE

COMPLETED
STORE FILES? :YES
STORED

RAN 1 SECONDS
*DELETE ALL
*LOAD FILRD

*10 FILES NEWSTK
*RUN


FILE   NEWSTK   LOADED
NUTS 4800   2500   1
WASHERS 250   200   1
NAILS 3650    4500   .5
HAMMERS 45   45   100
RIVETS 5000   3000   1
ENDFILE 0   0   0

COMPLETED
RAN 1 SECONDS
*
```

7·6   Program STKCPY

```
10 FILES NEWSTK,STOCK
20 DIM R$(10)
30 READ %1,1
40 LET N=0
50 READ %1;R$,R1,R2,R3
55 LET N=N+1
60 PRINT %2,N;R$,R1,R2,R3
65 IF R$ <>"ENDFILE" THEN 50
70 END
```

Section 7C: Digital Equipment Corporation – System 10

The following programs were run on the DEC System 10 at Hatfield Polytechnic.

7·1   Filed program manipulation

Input via the teleprinter keyboard is underlined.

```
LOGIN 300,102
JOA 42 503B PRIME TIME MONITOR TTY4
PASSWORD: _____
1052    29-JAN-72        SAT

.R BASIC
```

—For security, the password is not printed when typed at the teleprinter.

—The period indicates that the system is ready to receive a monitor command.

```
THIS VERSION OF 'BASIC' IS THE SAME AS THE OLD VERSION OF 'XBASIC'.
FOR DIFFERENCES LIST 'NEWS***'. IF YOU WISH TO
RUN YOUR PROGRAM UNDER THE OLD 'BASIC' YOU MAY DO SO BY
RUNNING 'XBASIC'.

16.5:BASIC    10:52         29-JAN-72
```

—Message of the day – information for anyone who logs in.

```
NEW OR OLD--NEW SUMS

READY
TAPE
```

—Informs the system that input is to be from tape.

```
READY

10 READ A,B,C,D,E,

20 PRINT A;B;C;D;E

30 PRINT A+B;B+C;C+D;D+E;E+A

40 DETA 10,20,25,12,16

KEY
```

—Informs the system that input is to continue from keyboard.

```
READY
RUN

SUMS          10:54          29-JAN-72


? ILLEGAL FORMAT IN 10
? ILLEGAL INSTRUCTION IN 40

? NO END INSTRUCTION

TIME:  0.04 SECS.
```

—Error messages.

```
READY
10 READ A,B,C,D,E
40 DATA 10,20,25,12,16
50 END
RUN
```

—Error correction.

```
SUMS            10:55        29-JAN-72
```
—*Successful run.*
```
 10   20   25   12   16
 30   45   37   28   26

TIME:   0.08 SECS.


READY
LIST
```
—*Command to list current program.*

```
SUMS            10:55        29-JAN-72

10 READ A,B,C,D,E
20 PRINT A;B;C;D;E
30 PRINT A+B;B+C;C+D;D+E;E+A
40 DATA 10,20,25,12,16
50 END

READY
SAVE
```
—*Copy program to file.*
```
READY
SCRATCH
```
—*Clear work space.*
```
READY
LIST
```
—*There is currently no program in the work space.*
```
SUMS            10:56        29-JAN-72


READY
OLD SUMS
```
—*Saved program SUMS is loaded into the work space.*
```
READY
RUN

SUMS            10:57        29-JAN-72


 10   20   25   12   16
 30   45   37   28   26


TIME:   0.08 SECS.


READY
CATALOG

TRYME  .BAS
LEARN  .BAS
ITSA   .BAS
FISHY  .BAS

TEST   .BAS
SUMS   .BAS
```
—*Library of programs saved under the present users password.*
```
READY
UNSAVE SUMS
```
—*Command to remove program SUMS from the saved programs library.*
```
READY
OLD SUMS
```
—*Attempt to get SUMS from library.*

```
? FILE NOT SAVED
READY
BYE                                                    —Sign off.
JOB 42, USER [300,102]  LOGGED OFF TTY4     1058  29-JAN-72
SAVED ALL 18 FILES (155. DISK BLOCKS)
RUNTIME 0 MIN, 01.56 SEC
```

7·2   Program FILCHK

```
5 FILES STOCK
20 INPUT I£
30 IF I£="FINISH" THEN 170
40 INPUT #1,R£,R1,R2,R3
50 IF R£="ENDFILE" THEN 150
60 IF I£<>R£ THEN 40
70 PRINT "ITEM ";R£;" STOCK IS ";R1
80 RESTORE #1
90 GOTO 20
150 PRINT "ITEM NOT IN STOCK"
155 RESTORE #1
160 GOTO 20
170 END
```

Statement 5   Specifies the data files to be used in the program.

Statement 40   Is interpreted as: read four items of data from the first named file. The items are a string and three numerics to be called *R£, R1, R2, R3*.

Statements 80 and 155   Are similar to the RESTORE statement used with a DATA statement. The pointer for file 1 is reset to the first item.

7·3   Program CREATE

```
NEW OR OLD--NEW CREATE

READY
10 FILES STOCK
20 SCRATCH #1
30 INPUT R£,R1,R2,R3
40 PRINT #1,R£,R1,R2,R3
50 IR=F R£<>"ENDFILE" THEN 30
60 END
SAVE

READY
```

The PRINT statement (40) causes the items listed to be read sequentially into file 1.

```
RUN

CREATE        11:02          29-JAN-72
```

```
?NUTS,5000,2500,1
?WASHERS,250,200,2
?NAILS,4000,4500,0.5
?HAMMERS,50,45,100
?RIVETS,5000,3000,1
?ENDFILE,0,0,0
```

```
TIME:   0.26 SECS.
```

7·4   Program CREUP

```
NEW CREUP

READY
10 FILES UPDATE
20 SCRATCH #1
30 INPUT R£,R1
40 PRINT #1,R£,R1
50 IF R£<>"ENDFILE----UP" THEN 30
60 END
RUN
```

```
CREUP              11:06            29-JAN-72
```

```
?NAILS,-200
?HAMMERS,-5
?NUTS,-200
?NAILS,-150
?ENDUP,0
```

```
TIME:   0.16 SECS.
```

7·5   Program STKUP

The program FILRD is also shown.

```
NEW FILRD

READY
10 FILES STUCK
20 INPUT #1,R£,R1,R2,R3
30 PRINT R£;R1;R2;R3
40 IF R£<>"ENDFILE" THEN 20
50 END
SAVE

READY
NEW STKUP

READY
10 FILES STUCK,UPDATE,NEWSTK
20 SCRATCH #3
30 INPUT #1,R£,R1,R2,R3
40 IF R£="ENDFILE" THEN 130
45 RESTORE#2
50 INPUT #2,S£,S1
60 IF R£<>S£ THEN 90
```

```
70 LET R1=R1+S1
80 GOTO 50
90 IF S£="ENDUP" THEN 110
100 GOTO 50
110 PRINT #3,R£,R1,R2,R3
120 GOTO 30
130 PRINT #3,"ENDFILE",0,0,0
140 END

SAVE

OLD FILRD

READY
RUN

FILRD           11:31         29-JAN-72


NUTS 5000   2500   1
WASHERS 250   200   2
NAILS 4000   4500  0.5
HAMMERS 50    45  100
RIVETS 5000   3000   1
ENDFILE 0   0   0


TIME:  0.18 SECS.

READY
OLD STKUP

READY
RUN

   STKUP           11:31         29-JAN-72


TIME:  0.30 SECS.

READY
OLD FILRD

READY
10 FILES NEWSTK
RUN

FILRD           11:32         29-JAN-72



NUTS 4800   2500   1
WASHERS 250   200   2
NAILS 4000   4500   0.5
HAMMERS 50    45  100
RIVETS 5000   3000   1
ENDFILE 0   0   0


TIME:  0.20 SECS.
```

7·6   Program STKCPY

```
NEW STKCPY

READY
10 FILES NEWSTK,STUCK
20 SCRATCH #2
30 INPUT #1,K£,K1,K2,K3
40 PRINT #2,K£,K1,K2,K3
50 IF K£<>"ENDFILE" THEN 30
60 END
SAVE
```

Section 7D: Hewlett-Packard 2000 Series

7·1 Filed program manipulation

Input via the teleprinter keyboard is underlined.

```
HELL0-D152,BHILLS
???
HELLO-D240,BHILL
ILLEGAL ACCESS
HELL0-D240,
```
—*Correct code number is D240.*

—*Password is typed after the comma. Printing is suppressed.*

```
ON AT 12:00  DECEMBER 12TH.,  1971
LEASCO RESPONSE 1 BASIC
OPEN UNIVERSITY STUDENTS - GET- AND RUN-$OPENU
```
—*Messages from system.*

```
TAPE
```
—*"I wish to load paper tape. No error messages until I have finished."*

```
10 READ A,B,C,D,E,
20 PRINT A;B;C;D;E
30 PRINT A+B;B+C;C+D;D+E;E+A
40 DETA 10,20,25,12,16
```

```
KEY
ILLEGAL READ VARIABLE  IN LINE 10
MISSING ASSIGNMENT OPERATOR  IN LINE 40
LAST INPUT IGNORED, RETYPE IT
```
—*"I have finished loading tape."*

—*Error messages*

```
10 READ A,B,C,D,E
40 DATA 10.20.----,20,25,12,16
```
—*New lines typed to correct errors.*

```
RUN
LAST STATEMENT NOT 'END' IN LINE 40
```
—*System command to run program.*
—*Run-time error message.*

```
50 END
NAME-SUMS
LIST
SUMS
```
—*Error corrected.*
—*Name current program.*
—*System command to list current program.*

```
10   READ A,B,C,D,E
20   PRINT A;B;C;D;E
30   PRINT A+B;B+C;C+D;D+E;E+A
40   DATA 10,20,25,12,16
50   END
SAVE
SCRATCH
LIST
```
—*Current program.*

—*Copy program to file.*
—*Clear work space.*
—*Attempt to list current program – no effect since work-space empty.*

```
GET-SUMS
RUN
SUMS     1203
```
—*Copy SUMS from file to work space.*

—*Time of day.*

```
10     20     25     12     16
30     45     37     28     26
```
—*Output from program.*

169

```
DONE AT 1203
CATALOG
A/1    -UP-00064-279/71   A/2    -UP-00119-188/71   A/3    -UP-00169-188/71
F/7    -UP-00370-279/71   F/8    -UP-00352-279/71   SUMS   -UP-00047-346/71
```
Catalogue of users private library and space occupied.

<u>KILL-SUMS</u>   *—Remove SUMS from library.*

<u>GET-SUMS</u>
<u>NO SUCH</u> PROGRAM   *—Attempt to get SUMS from library.*

<u>BYE</u>   *—Signing off.*
004 MINUTES OF TERMINAL TIME

OFF AT 12:04

7·2   Program FILCHK

Based on the earlier program STKCHK.

```
FILCHK

5   FILES STOCK
10    DIM I$[10],R$[10]
20    INPUT I$
30    IF I$="FINISH" THEN 170
40    READ #1;R$,R1,R2,R3
50    IF R$="ENDFILE" THEN 150
60    IF I$ <> R$ THEN 40
70    PRINT "ITEM ";R$;" STOCK IS ";R1
80    READ #1,1
90    GOTO 20
150    PRINT "ITEM NOT IN STOCK"
155    READ #1,1
160    GOTO 20
170    END
```

Statement 5   Specifies the data files to be used in the program.

Statement 40   Is interpreted as: read four items of data from the first named file in the FILES list. The items are a string and three numerics and are to be called *R$*, *R1*, *R2*, *R3*.

Statements 80 and 155 Have a similar action to RESTORE. When reading data from a file sequentially, a pointer keeps check on which item is to be read next.

                         READ #1, *N* has the effect of setting the pointer to the *N*th record so that sequential reading will begin from there.

7·3   Program CREATE

```
LIST
CREATE

10    FILES STOCK
20    DIM R$[10]
30    LET N=1
40    INPUT R$,R1,R2,R3
50    PRINT #1,N;R$,R1,R2,R3
60    LET N=N+1
70    IF R$#"ENDFILE" THEN 40
80    END
```

Note that the use of PRINT #1, N; (variable names) allows a particular record to be referenced. If ",N" were omitted, the items would simply be stored sequentially in the records, automatically moving onto the next record when the previous one is filled.

Before program CREATE can be run an area on disc has to be reserved for the data file (similar to the DIM statement). This is done by the system command OPEN as shown in the printout.

```
OPEN-STOCK,10


RUN
CREATE   1247

?"NUTS",5000,2500,1
?"WASHERS",250,200,2
?"NAILS",4000,4500,0.5
?"HAMMERS",50,45,100
?"RIVETS",5000,3000,1
?"ENDFILE",0,0,0

DONE AT 1248
```

7·4   Program CREUP

```
CREUP

10    FILES UPDATE
20    DIM R$[10]
30    LET N=1
40    INPUT R$,R1
50    PRINT #1,N;R$,R1
60    LET N=N+1
70    IF R$ <> "ENDUP" THEN 40
80    END


RUN
CREUP    1351

?"NAILS",-200
?"HAMMERS",-5
?"NUTS",-200
?"NAILS",-150
?"ENDUP",0

DONE AT 1352
```

7·5   Program STKUP

```
STKUP

10    FILES STOCK,UPDATE,NEWSTK
20    READ #1,1
30    LET N=0
40    DIM R$[10],S$[10]
50    READ #1;R$,R1,R2,R3
55    LET N=N+1
60    IF R$="ENDFILE" THEN 160
70    READ #2,1
80    READ #2;S$,S1
90    IF R$ <> S$ THEN 120
100    LET R1=R1+S1
110    GOTO 80
120    IF S$="ENDUP" THEN 140
130    GOTO 80
140    PRINT #3,N;R$,R1,R2,R3
150    GOTO 50
160    PRINT #3,N;"ENDFILE",0,0,0
170    END


GET-FILRD
```

```
RUN
FILRD    1436

NUTS 5000        2500        1
WASHERS 250      200      2
NAILS 400        4500         .5
HAMMERS 50       45       100
RIVETS 5000         3000         1
ENDFILE 0        0        0

DONE AT 1436


GET-STKUP
RUN
STKUP    1437


DONE AT 1437
GET-FILRD
10 FILES NEWSTK
RUN
FILRD    1437

NUTS 4800        2500        1
WASHERS 250      200      2
NAILS 50         4500         .5
HAMMERS 45       45       100
RIVETS 5000         3000         1
ENDFILE 0        0        0

DONE AT 1437
```

7·6   Program STKCPY

```
10    FILES NEWSTK,STOCK
20    DIM R$[10]
30    READ #1,1
40    LET N=0
50    READ #1;R$,R1,R2,R3
55    LET N=N+1
60    PRINT #2,N;R$,R1,R2,R3
65    IF R$#"ENDFILE" THEN 50
70    END
```

Section 7E: Honeywell Time Sharing

7·1 Filed program manipulation

Input via the teleprinter keyboard is underlined.

```
ON AT  17:10    G265 B 07/08/72   TTY  6

USER NUMBER--36998
INCORRECT FORMAT - RETYPE IT--B36998
SYSTEM--BASIC                          —Call up BASIC compiler
NEW OR OLD--NEW
NEW FILE NAME--SUMS                     —New program, to be called SUMS.
READY.

TAPE                                    —System command to receive input
READY.                                   from tape reader on the teleprinter.

10 READ A,B,C,D,E,
20 PRINT A;B;C;D;E
30 PRINT A+B;B+C;C+D;D+E;E+A
40 DETA 10,20,25,12,16
KEY                                     —Revert to keyboard entry.
READY.

RUN                                     —System command to RUN program.

SUMS       17:12    G265 B 07/08/72


INCORRECT  FORMAT     IN   40           —Error message.


USED    0.67 UNITS.
40 DATA 10,20,25,12,16                  —Error corrected.
LIST                                    —System command to LIST current
                                         program.

SUMS       17:12    G265 B 07/08/72

10 READ A,B,C,D,E,
20 PRINT A;B;C;D;E
30 PRINT A+B;B+C;C+D;D+E;E+A
40 DATA 10,20,25,12,16

SAVE                                    —Copy program to file.

READY.

SCRATCH                                 —Clear work space.
READY.

LIST                                    —Work space is empty.
NO FILE.

OLD SUMS                                —Copy SUMS from file to work space.

READY.

RUN
```

175

```
SUMS        17:13    G265 B 07/08/72
```

10	20	25	12	16
30	45	37	28	26

—Output from program.

```
USED      1.50 UNITS.
CATALOGUE
```

—Request for catalogue of user's private library.

```
SAVED FILES, USER NUMBER B36998
G265 B 07/08/72 72220 TIME: 17:13
```

```
TALK     CREATE   RKINET: USLIST: PRINTS   CREUP    STKCPY
FILCHK   STKUP    STOCK   UPDATE  FILRD    NEWSTK   SUMS
```

```
READY.
```

```
UNSAVE SUMS
```

—Remove SUMS from library.

```
READY.
```

```
OLD SUMS
```

—Attempt to get SUMS from library.

```
FILE NOT SAVED--SUMS
```

```
BYE
```

—Signing off.

```
*** OFF AT 17:13   G265 B 07/08/72

    3 ELAPSED TERMINAL MINUTES

    2.17 TOTAL CRU'S USED
```

7·2   Program FILCHK

Based on the earlier program STKCHK.

```
5 FILES STOCK
20 INPUT I£
30 IF I£="FINISH" THEN 170
40 READ:1,R£,R1,R2,R3
50 IF R£="ENDFILE" THEN 150
60 IF I£<>R£ THEN 40
70 PRINT "ITEM ";R£;" STOCK IS ";R1
80 RESTORE:1
90 GOTO 20
150 PRINT "ITEM NOT IN STOCK"
155 RESTORE:1
160 GOTO 20
170 END
```

Statement 5   Specifies the files used by the program.

Statement 40   Is interpreted as: read four items of data from file 1 (file 1 is the first named file in the FILES list and is referenced   :1). The items are a string and three numerics and are to be called *R£*, *R1*, *R2* and *R3*.

Statements 80 and 155   Both have a similar action to the RESTORE statement introduced earlier. RESTORE:1 moves the pointer for file 1 back to the first item in the file. It should be noted that a string variable occupies three locations in the file. Thus after reading the first *R£*, *R1*, *R2*, *R3*, the pointer will be at location 7.

The pointer may be set to any location in the file by using SET:1, N , which sets the pointer for file 1 to the NIL location.

7·3   Program CREATE

```
CREATE     15:48    G265 B 05/08/72

10  FILES STOCK
20  INPUT R£,R1,R2,R3
30  WRITE:1,R£;R1;R2;R3
40  IF R£<>"ENDFILE" THEN 20
50  END
```

Before CREATE can be run, a storage area on disc must be reserved to hold the file STOCK. The system library contains six file 'outlines' of different sizes. To reserve storage area, one of these 'outline' files must be obtained, renamed as required (in this case STOCK) and saved in the user library. The six files in the system library are:

CH0192***   CH0384***   CH0768***
CH1536***   CH3072***   CH6144***

the number in each being the number of characters which may be held on that file.

```
OLD CH0384***


READY.

RENAME STOCK
READY.

SAVE


READY.

RUN CREATE


CREATE     15:50    G265 B 05/08/72

? NUTS,5000,2500,1
? WASHERS,250,200,2
```

```
? NAILS,4000,4500,0.5
? HAMMERS,50,45,100
? RIVETS,5000,3000,1
? ENDFILE,0,0,0
```

7·4   Program CREUP

```
CREUP      15:54    G265 B 05/08/72

10 FILES UPDATE
40 INPUT R£,R1
50 WRITE:1,R£,R1
70 IF R£<>"ENDUP" THEN 40
80 END

OLD CH0384***


READY.

RENAME UPDATE
READY.

SAVE


READY.

RUN CREUP


CREUP      15:55    G265 B 05/08/72

? NAILS,-200
? HAMMERS,-5
? NUTS,-200
? NAILS,-150
? ENDUP,0
```

7·5   Program STKUP

CH0384*** is again renamed (NEWSTK). This
is omitted from the following printout:

```
STKUP      16:04    G265 B 05/08/72

10 FILES STOCK,UPDATE,NEWSTK
50 READ:1,R£,R1,R2,R3
60 IF R£="ENDFILE" THEN 160
70 RESTORE:2
80 READ:2,S£,S1
90 IF R£<>S£ THEN 120
100 LET R1=R1+S1
110 GOTO 80
120 IF S£="ENDUP" THEN 140
130 GOTO 80
140 WRITE:3,R£,R1,R2,R3
150 GOTO 50
160 WRITE:3,"ENDFILE",0,0,0
170 END
```

In the following program runs, units of computer time used have been omitted.

```
OLD FILRD

READY.

RUN


FILRD      16:06     G265 B 05/08/72

NUTS 5000   2500   1
WASHERS 250     200    2
NAILS 4000   4500   .5
HAMMERS 50      45      100
RIVETS 5000   3000   1
ENDFILE 0   0    0



USED      3.33 UNITS.
OLD STKUP

READY.

RUN


STKUP      16:06     G265 B 05/08/72



USED      5.00 UNITS.
OLD FILRD

READY.

10 FILES NEWSTK
RUN


FILRD      16:07     G265 B 05/08/72

NUTS 4800,  2500   1
WASHERS 250     200    2
NAILS 3650   4500   .5
HAMMERS 45      45      100
RIVETS 5000   3000   1
ENDFILE 0   0    0
```

7·6   Program STKCPY

```
10 FILES NEWSTK,STOCK
50 READ:2,R£,R1,R2,R3
60 WRITE:1,R£,R1,R2,R3
65 IF R£<>"ENDFILE" THEN 50
70 END
```

Section 7F: IBM — CALL/360

7·1 Filed program manipulation

Input via the teleprinter keyboard is underlined.

```
LINE 56
ON AT 10:32   06/10/72  FRIDAY
NEW BASIC COURSES ARRANGED - PLEASE RUN ***COURSES          —Message from system.
USER NUMBER,PASSWORD--ABC124,DAVID
USER NUMBER,PASSWORD--ABC124,PETER        ⎤—Correct password was PETER.
READY

NAME SUMS
READY

10 READ A,B,C,D,E,
20 PRINT A;B;C;D;E
30 PRINT USING 40,A+B,B+C,C+D,D+E,E+A
40: ##  ####    ##.## ##     ##.##        —Image statement specifying a format
50 DETA 10,20,25,12,16                      picture for line 30.

RUN                                        — System command to RUN program.

SUMS        10:36  10/06/72  FRIDAY   UK2

LINE   10:   SYNTAX ERROR IN STATEMENT
LINE   50:   SYNTAX ERROR IN STATEMENT    ⎤
LINE   50:   END STATEMENT MISSING         —Error messages.
COMPILATION TERMINATED                     ⎦

TIME    0 SECS.

REP 10,'E,','E'                            —Replace E, of statement 10 by E.
READY

REP 'DETA','DATA'                          —Replace all occurrences of DETA by
READY                                        DATA.

60 END

RUN

SUMS        10:37  10/06/72  FRIDAY   UK2

10    20    25    12    16
30    45    37.00 28    26.00

TIME    0 SECS.

LIS H                                      —System command to list current pro-
10 READ A,B,C,D,E                            gram without headings.
20 PRINT A;B;C;D;E
30 PRINT USING 40,A+B,B+C,C+D,D+E,E+A
40: ##  ####    ##.## ##     ##.##
50 DATA 10,20,25,12,16
60 END

SAV                                        —Copy program to file.
READY

CLE                                        —Clear work space.
READY
```

181

```
LIS
NO PROGRAM PRESENT
```
]— *Current work space is empty.*

```
LOA SUMS
READY
```
—*Load SUMS from file into work space.*

```
RUN

SUMS          10:39   10/06/72   FRIDAY        UK2

  10     20     25    12    16
  30     45     37.00  28    26.00

TIME      0 SECS.
```

```
PUR SUMS
READY
```
—*Remove SUMS from file using PURGE command.*

```
LOA SUMS
SUMS NOT SAVED
```
—*Attempt to retrieve SUMS from file.*

```
OFF
OFF AT 10:40
PROC. TIME...    0 SEC.
TERM. TIME...   10 MIN.
```
—*Signing off.*

7·2   Program FILCHK

Based on the earlier program STKCHK.

```
LOA FILCHK
READY

LIS H
10 OPEN 1,'STOCK',INPUT
20 DIM I£(10),R£(10)
25 INPUT I£
30 IF I£='FINISH' GOTO 170
40 GET 1:R£,R1,R1,R3
50 IF R£='ENDFILE'GOTO150
60 IF I£<>R£ GOTO 40
70 PRINT 2'ITEM '; R£;' STOCK IS'; R1
80 RESET 1
90 GOTO 25
150 PRINT 'ITEM NOT IN STORE'
160 RESET 1
165 GOTO 20
170 CLOSE 1
180 END
```

Statement 10   Specifies the data file to be used, specifying input mode.

Statement 40   Is interpreted as: read four items of data from the first file. These items are a string and three numerics to be called $R\$$, $R1$, $R2$ and $R3$.

Statements 80 and 160   Have a similar action to RESTORE with DATA statements. RESET 1 moves the pointer for file 1 back to the first item in the file.

7·3   Program CREATE

```
CLE
READY

LOA CREATE
READY

LIS H
10 OPEN 1,'STOCK',OUTPUT
20 INPUT R£,R1,R2,R3
30 PUT 1:R£,R1,R2,R3
40 IF R£='ENDFILE' GOTO 60
50 GOTO20
60 CLOSE 1
70 END
```

File STOCK is to be in output mode.

Statement 30 Causes the values of *R£, R1, R2, R3* to be written into data file 1.

```
RUN

CREATE      10:44   10/06/72  FRIDAY      UK2

?   'NUTS',5000,2500,1
?   'WASHERS',250,200,2
?   'NAILS',4000,4500,0.5
?   'HAMMERS',50,45,100
?   'RIVETS',5000,3000,1
?   'ENDFILE',0,0,0

TIME      0 SECS.


CLE
READY
```

7·4   Program CREUP

Note: in this and the programs which follow, the file AMEND corresponds to the file UPDATE of chapter 7.

```
LOA CREUP
READY

LIS H
10 OPEN 2,'AMEND',OUTPUT
20 INPUT S£,S1
30 PUT 2:S£,S1
40 IF S£='ENDFILE' GOTO 60
50 GOTO 20
60 CLOSE 2
70 END
```

```
NAME AMEND
READY


10 'NAILS',-200
20 'HAMMERS',-5
30 'NUTS',-200
40 'NAILS',-150
50 'ENDFILE',0

SAV
READY


CLE
READY
```

7·5   Program STKUP

```
LOA STKUP
READY


LIS H
10 OPEN 1,'STOCK',INPUT
20 OPEN 2,'AMEND',INPUT
30 OPEN 3,'NWSTK',OUTPUT
40 GET 1:R£,R1,R2,R3
50 IF R£='ENDFILE' GOTO 160
60 GET 2:S£,S1
70 IF S£='ENDFILE' GOTO 120
80 IF S£=R£ GOTO 100
90 GOTO 60
100 LET R1=R1+S1
110 GOTO60
120 PUT 3:R£,R1,R2,R3
130 PRINT R£,R1,R2,R3
140 RESET 2
150 GOTO 40
160 CLOSE 1,2,3
170 END
```

The PRINT statement in line 130 is used instead of the more general FILRD program of Chapter 7.

```
RUN

STKUP        10:52    10/06/72   FRIDAY       UK2

NUTS                  4800            2500            1
WASHERS               250             200             2
NAILS                 3650            4500            .5
HAMMERS               45              45              100
RIVETS                5000            3000            1

TIME      0 SECS.
```

7·6   Program STKCPY

```
CLE
READY


LOA STKCPY
READY


LIS H
10 OPEN 1,'NWSTK',INPUT
20 OPEN 2,'STOCK',OUTPUT
30 GET 1:R£,R1,R2,R3
40 IF R£='ENDFILE' GOTO 80
50 PUT 2:R£,R1,R2,R3
60 PRINT R£,R1,R2,R3
70 GOTO 30
80 CLOSE 1,2
90 END


SAV
READY


RUN

STKCPY       10:55    10/06/72   FRIDAY       UK2

NUTS                  4800            2500            1
WASHERS               250             200             2
NAILS                 3650            4500            .5
HAMMERS               45              45              100
RIVETS                5000            3000            1

LINE    30:   END OF FILE

TIME      0 SECS.


OFF
OFF AT 10:56
PROC. TIME...    0 SEC.
TERM. TIME...   14 MIN.
```

Section 7G: ICL – 1900 Series

This version of BASIC is for systems operating under the GEORGE 3 operating system. The printout shown is edited from a longer session and times should be ignored.

7·1 Filed program manipulation

Input via the teleprinter keyboard is underlined.

```
THIS IS GEORGE 3 MARK 7.1 ON 21NOV72
08.43.11- LN MOPBSA,:T344SCHOOLS
STARTED :T344SCHOOLS,MOPBSA,21NOV72  08.44.23 TYPE:MOP
08.44.30- JD 6,10000
08.44.54- BASIC
WAITING AS DIRECTED
08.46.58 0.01 USED URGENCY M
08.46.59 JOB IS NOW FULLY STARTED
08.48.27 0.02 CORE GIVEN 7232
BASIC SYSTEM MARK 1A
NEW OR OLD?
- NEW SUMS
- 10 READ A,B,C,D,E,
VARIABLE MUST START WITH A LETTER
10 READ A,B,C,D,E,
                  '
- 10 READ A,B,C,D,E
- 20 PRINT A;B;C;D;E
- 30 PRINT A+B;B+C;C+E;--D;D+E;E+A
- 40 DETA 10,20,25,12,16
STATEMENT NAME NOT RECOGNISED
40 DETA 10,20,25,12,16
       '
- 40 DATA 10,20,25,12,16
- RUN
              RUN PROCEEDING
  10    20    25    12    16
  30    45    37    28    26

              FINISHED
- LIST

SUMS          ON 21/11/72 AT 12.21.39

10 READ A,B,C,D,E
20 PRINT A;B;C;D;E
30 PRINT A+B;B+C;C+D;D+E;E+A
40 DATA 10,20,25,12,16

- SAVE
- SCRATCH
- LIST
PROGRAM FILE IS EMPTY-COMMAND ABANDONED
- OLD SUMS
- RUN
              RUN PROCEEDING
  10    20    25    12    16
  30    45    37    28    26
```

Entry of user's 'log in' code. On many systems, the user is then asked for a password.
—Allocation of core storage.
—Request for BASIC system.

—Messages from the system as BASIC is loaded and brought on line.

—Is a new or a filed program required?
—User names a new program SUMS.

—Error detected by the system and corrected by the user.

—Error detected by the system and corrected by the user.

—Successful program run.

—Listing of current program.

—Program filed.
—Work space cleared.
—There is no current program.
—Load file 'SUMS' into work space.

187

```
                 FINISHED
- UNSAVE SUMS                            —Remove 'SUMS' from file.
- OLD SUMS
PROGRAM SUMS DOES NOT EXIST              —'SUMS' is no longer on file.

- BYE
WAITING AS DIRECTED                      —BASIC system is deleted and control
END OF MACRO                              is returned to the GEORGE operating
12.33.40- LD                              system.

   LISTDIR LISTING OF DIRECTORY      :T344SCHOOLS

   TYPE     NAME      GEN.NO. LANG.   REEL.NO.  SERIAL NO.

FILE      CONTROLFILE      1
FILE      LABASOURCE       1
FILE      LABESOURCE       1
                                         —List of files under user's code. Only
                                          part of the actual list is shown.
FILE      MOPBSA           1    C1
FILE      NEWSTK           1
FILE      PARAS            1
FILE      STKUP            1    BSIC

12.41.04- LT                             —Logout command.
MAXIMUM ONLINE BS USED 31 KWORDS
12.41.53 0.37 FINISHED :T344SCHOOLS,MOPBSA : 0 LISTFILES

     SWITCH OFF TELETYPE NOW
```

7·2   Program FILCHK

Based on the earlier program STKCHK.

```
5 FILES STOCK
20 INPUT I$
30 IF I$="FINISH" THEN 170
40 READ #1,R$,R1,R2,R3
50 IF R$="ENDFILE" THEN 150
60 IF I$<>R$ THEN 40
70 PRINT "ITEM ";R$;" STOCK IS ";R1
80 RESTORE #1
90 GO TO 20
150 PRINT "ITEM NOT IN STOCK"
155 RESTORE #1
160 GO TO 20
170 END
```

Statement 5   Specifies the data files to be used in the program.

Statement 40   Is interpreted as: read four items of data from the first named file in the FILES list. The items are a string and three numerics to be called $R\$$, $R1$, $R2$, $R3$.

Statements 80 and 155   Both have a similar action to the RESTORE statement associated with DATA statements. When reading data from a file sequentially, a pointer keeps check on which item is to be read next.

7·3 Program CREATE

```
- OLD CREATE
- LIST

CREATE          ON 21/11/72 AT 10.22.40

10 FILES STOCK
20 SCRATCH #1
30 INPUT R$,R1,R2,R3
40 WRITE #1,R$,R1,R2,R3
50 IF R$<>"ENDFILE" THEN 30
60 END
```

The SCRATCH statement causes the specified file to be set to the 'write' mode. Subsequent WRITE statements (such as statement 40) then write data starting at the beginning of the file overwriting any previous contents.

In the RUN which follows, it will be noted that the familiar ' ? ' in response to INPUT is replaced by the statement number of the INPUT statement and the number of items to be entered.

```
- RUN
            RUN PROCEEDING

          30     INPUT  4
- "NUTS",5000,2500,1

          30     INPUT  4
- "WASHERS",250,200,2

          30     INPUT  4
- "NAIL",4000,4500,0.5

          30     INPUT  4
- "HAMMERS",50,45,100

          30     INPUT  4
- "RIVETS",5000,3500,1

          30     INPUT  4
- "ENDFILE",0,0,0

            FINISHED
```

7·4   Program CREUP

```
- OLD CREUP
- LIST

CREUP          ON 21/11/72 AT 10.31.51

10 FILES UPDATE
20 SCRATCH #1
30 INPUT R$,R1
40 WRITE #1,R$,R1
50 IF R$<>"ENDUP" THEN 30
60 END

- RUN
          RUN PROCEEDING

        30     INPUT  2
- "NAILS", -200

        30     INPUT  2
- "HAMMERS", -5

        30     INPUT  2
- "NUTS", -200

        30     INPUT  2
- "NAILS", -150

        30     INPUT  2
- "ENDUP", 0

             FINISHED
```

7·5   Program STKUP

```
- OLD STKUP
- LIST

STKUP          ON 21/11/72 AT 10.42.39

10 FILES STOCK,UPDATE,NEWSTK
15 SCRATCH #3
20 RESTORE #1
30 READ #1,R$,R1,R2,R3
40 IF R$="ENDFILE" THEN 140
50 RESTORE #2
60 READ #2,S$,S1
70 IF R$<>S$ THEN 100
80 LET R1=R1+S1
90 GO TO 60
100 IF S$="ENDUP" THEN 120
110 GO TO 60
120 WRITE #3, R$,R1,R2,R3
130 GO TO 30
140 WRITE #3,"ENDFILE",0,0,0
150 END

- OLD FILRD
- RUN
```

```
                 RUN  PROCEEDING
NUTS              5000    2500   1
WASHERS           250     .200   2
NAILS             4000    4500   .5
HAMMERS           50      45     100
RIVETS            5000    3500   1
ENDFILE           0    0    0


                 FINISHED
- OLD STKUP
- RUN
                 RUN  PROCEEDING

                 FINISHED
- OLD FILRD
- 10 FILES NEWSTK
- RUN

                 RUN  PROCEEDING
NUTS              4800    2500   1
WASHERS           250     200    2
NAILS             3650    4500   .5
HAMMERS           45      45     100
RIVETS            5000    3500   1
ENDFILE           0    0    0

                 FINISHED
- LIST

FILRD          ON 21/11/72 AT 11.59.24

10 FILES NEWSTK
20 READ #1,R$,R1,R2,R3
30 PRINT R$,R1;R2;R3
40 IF R$<>"ENDFILE" THEN 20
50 END
```

The program FILRD is shown above with statement 10 changed to FILES NEWSTK. Before this change, the statement was 10 FILES STOCK.

7.6   Program STKCPY

```
- OLD STKP-CPY
- LIST

STKCPY         ON 21/11/72 AT 12.04.30

10 FILES NEWSTK,STOCK
20 SCRATCH#2
30 READ #1,R$,R1,R2,R3
40 WRITE#2,R$,R1,R2,R3
50 IF R$<>"ENDFILE" THEN 30
60 END
```

Section 7H : ICL – System 4

This version of System 4 BASIC was developed and is supplied by J. Harwell Data Processing Ltd.

7·1 Filed program manipulation

Input via the teleprinter keyboard is underlined.

```
AUTOMAN   19/10/73   11:45:39   <17/00000/026>   T4
USER NUMBER ?
3
PASSWORD ?                                        —Printing of password is suppressed.
SYSTEM ?
BASIC
NEW OR OLD JOB ?
NEW
PROBLEM NAME ?
SUMS
READY
10 READ A,B,C,D,E,
ILLEGAL INSTRUCTION FORMAT                        —Error messages follow immediately.
10 READ A,B,C.⌴,D,E                               —Underline deletes the last character
20 PRINT A;B;C;D;E                                 typed.
30 PRINT A+B;B+C;C+D;D+E;E+A
40 DETA 10,20,25,12,16                            If the paper tape reader is on and
INVALID/ABSENT KEYWORD                            loaded, the tape is accepted auto-
40 DATA 10,20,25,12,16                            matically – no command needed.
RUN
END NOT LAST STATEMENT, IN LINE 40               —Run-time error.
50 WND
CA
50 END                                            —Control-X cancels an entire message.
LIST
SUMS      19/10/73   11:48
10 READ A,B,C,D,E
20 PRINT A;B;C;D;E
30 PRINT A+B;B+C;C+D;D+E;E+A
40 DATA 10,20,25,12,16
50 END


SAVE
CATALOG
  CREATE
  CREUP
  STKUP
  FILCHK
  STKCPY
  SUMS
COPY SUM                                          —Takes a copy under the name SUM.
UNSAVE SUMS                                       —Deletes SUMS from the disc.
SCRATCH                                           —Clears current file.
READY
LIS                                               —Any command may be abbreviated
NO LINES                                           to 3 letters.
OLD
PROBLEM NAME ?
SUM                                               —Transfers to program SUM.
READY
```

193

```
RUN
SUM       19/10/73   11:50
10   20   25   12   16
30   45   37   28   26
```
                                              —*Program output.*

```
READY
OLD
PROBLEM NAME ?
SUMS
OLD NAME NOT ON INDEX,RESTATE NEW OR OLD
GOODBYE
TIME:00.05.27,CPU UNITS:2560
```
                                              —*Signing off*

7·2   Program FILCHK

Based on the earlier program STKCHK.

```
OLD
PROBLEM NAME ?
FILCHK
READY
LIST
FILCHK  19/10/73   11:52
10 FILES 1
20 IF END #1 THEN 150
30 INPUT IS
40 IF IS='FINISH' THEN 170
50 READ #1,RS,R1,R2,R3
60 IF IS<>RS THEN 50
70 PRINT USING 80,RS,R1
80:ITEM "XXXXXXXX" STOCK IS######
90 RESTORE #1
100 GO TO 30
150 PRINT "ITEM NOT IN STOCK."
155 RESTORE #1
160 GOTO 30
170 END
```

Statement 10	Specifies the data file to be used in the program. All other data files are deleted.
Statement 20	Nominates the statement to which control is transferred whenever end-of-file is encountered reading file 1.
Statement 50	Reads a string and three numbers from file 1.
Statement 80	Defines the format in which $R\$$ and $R1$ are to be printed.
Statements 90 and 155	Reset the pointer for file 1 so that the next READ #1 will reread from the beginning. This is automatic when a program starts running.

7·3   Program CREATE

```
OLD
PROBLEM NAME ?
CREATE
READY
LIST
CREATE   19/10/73   11:53
10 FILES 1
20 INPUT R$,R1,R2,R3
30 IF R$='ENDFILE' THEN 60
40 WRITE#1,R$,R1,R2,R3
50 GOTO 20
60 END
RUN
CREATE _ 19/10/73   11:54
?
NUTS,5000,2500,1
?
WASHERS,250,200,2
?
NAILS,4000,4500,0.5
?
HAMMERS,50,45,100
?
RIVETS,5000,3000,1
?
ENDFILE

READY
```

—Apostrophes are not needed for strings beginning with a letter, input at run time.

—Zeros are implied for the last three variables.

Statement 40 Writes the values of $R\$$, $R1$, $R2$, $R3$ to file 1 following all existing data in the file.

7·4   Program CREUP

```
OLD
PROBLEM NAME ?
CREUP
READY
LIST
CREUP   19/10/73   11:56
10 FILES 1,2
20 SCRATCH #2
30 INPUT R$,R1
40 IF R$='ENDUP' THEN 70
50 WRITE #2,R$,R1
60 GOTO 30
70 END
RUN
CREUP   19/10/73   11:56
?
NAILS,-200
?
HAMMERS,-5
?
NUTS,-200
?
```

```
NAILS,-150
?
ENDUP

READY
```

Statement 20 Deletes all the data currently in
               file 2.

7.5   Program STKUP

```
OLD
PROBLEM NAME ?
STKUP
READY
LIST
STKUP    19/10/73   11:58
10 FILES 1,2,3
20 IF END #2 THEN 90
30 READ #1,R$,R1,R2,R3
40 RESTORE#2
50 READ #2,S$,S1
60 IF R$<>S$ THEN 50
70 R1=R1+S1
80 GOTO 50
90 WRITE #3,R$,R1,R2,R3
100 GOTO 30
110 END
```

Since there is no IF END # 1 statement, the
program will end when it reaches the end of
file 1.

7.6   Program STKCPY

```
OLD
PROBLEM NAME ?
STKCPY
READY
LIST
STKCPY 19/10/73   11:59
10 FILES 1,3
20 SCRATCH #1
30 READ #3,R$,R1,R2,R3
40 WRITE #1,R$,R1,R2,R3
50 GOTO 30
60 END
```

Section 7I: Rank Xerox Data Systems SIGMA 5-9

7·1 Filed program manipulation

Input via the teleprinter keyboard is underlined.

```
UTS AT YOUR SERVICE
ON AT 1630  OCT 18,72
LOGON PLEASE:   04B2,FR
ACCOUNT/ID 04B2,FR?
LOGON PLEASE:   0462,FRED,


16:31    08/10/72      0462 FRED


!BASIC


>10 PAE--EAD A,B,C,D,E
>20 PRINT A;B;C;D;E
>30 ;A+B;B+C;C+D;D+E;E+A
>40 DATA 20,30,40,
40 DATA 10,20,30,---
40 DATA 10,20,25,12,16
>SAVE ON JS1
>CLEAR
>LIST
  NO PROGRAM


>LOAD JS1
>LIST
10 READ A,B,C,D,E
20 PRINT A;B;C;D;E
30 ;A+B;B+C;C+D;D+E;E+A
40 DATA 10,20,25,12,16
>RUN
16:48    OCT 19   JS3
  10     20     25     12     16
  30     45     37     28     26


      40 HALT
>CLEAR


>10 INPUT A,B,C
>20 A=X*4,B=Y+C
>30 ;A,B,C,X;Y;Z
>;200*57
 11400
>40 ;"END OF TEST"


>REN 60,10,5
>LIST
60 INPUT A,B,C
65 A=X*4,B=Y+C
70 ;A,B,C,X;Y;Z
75 ;"END OF TEST"
>
```

19-4 (1)

Correct account number and name is 0462, FRED.

Password is typed after command. Echo is suppressed.

— *User requests the BASIC processor.*

— *Error correction in first line (10) of program.*
— *First ; is equivalent to PRINT*
Line cancelled by typing (ESC)X.
—*Type (ESC) R, then complete line.*
—*Program name JS1. 'SAVE ON' saves the program only for the current session.*
— *Workspace has been cleared, hence there is no current program to list.*

— *Workspace loaded with program JS1.*

—*Time of day and date printed as part of the response to the RUN command.*

— *Line number of final statement executed.*

— *Entry of new program.*

— *BASIC used in desk calculator mode during the entry of a program.*

—*User asks for statements to be renumbered.*

197

```
>EXE60-70                              —EXECUTE command to test part
?4,6,9                                                       program.
 0               9              9              0      0

        70 EXECUTE HALT
>WEAVE JS1                             —WEAVE command, brings old pro-
>RUN                                   gram JS1 to workspace. The two
16:56    OCT 18   JS1                  programs are now run as one.
  10    20    25    12    16
  30    45    37    28    26
?3,56,7
  0              7              7              0   0   0
END OF TEST

       75 HALT
>SAVE OVER JS2                         — Program named as JS2 and saved.
>DEL JS1                               —JS1 deleted. Since this was saved with
                                        a SAVE ON command, deletion
>SYS                                    would have taken place when logging
                                        off.
!BYE
                                       User exits from BASIC and logs out.
18/10/'72 16:57
LOG ON TIME 23
RAD SPACE 2
6OM TIME 0.136
```

7·2   Program FILCHK

Based on the earlier program STKCHK.

```
10 OPEN "STOCK" ,TO 1,INPUT
20 INPUT I$
30 IF I$="FINISH" THEN 130
40 INPUT:1,R$,R1,R2,R3
50 ENDFILE:1,100
60 IF I$<>R$ THEN 40
70 ;"ITEM";R$;"STOCK IS";R1
80 INPUT:1;1
90 GOTO 20
100 ;"ITEM NOT IN STOCK"
110 INPUT:1;1
120 GOTO 20
130 END
```

Statement 10	Opens the file labelled 'STOCK', connects it to stream 1 and indicates that the program will input information from the file.
Statement 40	Asks for four items from the file opened on stream 1. 'INPUT' is used in the case of BCD files, 'GET' in the case of binary files.
Statement 50	Tells the program to branch to statement 100 on an out of data condition (i.e. End of File) on stream 1. The word 'Endfile' is a command and is not physically stored in the file.
Statements 80 and 110	Both have a similar action to RESTORE. The number (or variable) after the ; is the number of the record to which the pointer is to be reset and from which sequential reading will begin.

7·3   Program CREATE

```
10 OPEN "STOCK" TO 1,PRINT OVER
20 N=1
30 INPUT R$,R1,R2,R3
40 IF R$="ENDFILE" THEN 80
50 ;:1;N,R$,R1,R2,R3
60 N=N+1
70 GOTO 30
80 END
```

Statement 10 Opens file 'STOCK', connects it to stream 1 and indicates that the program will write information into it, overwriting all old information if any. PRINT is used with BCD files, PUT with binary files.

Statement 50 Lists the stream number, record number (N) and four variables to be written into that record. ; is the shorthand equivalent of PRINT.

```
>LOAD CREATE
>
!TABS 20,30,40

!PROCEED

        BASIC RESTORED
>RUN
09:23   OCT 20   CREATE
?NUTS              5000        2500         1
?WASHERS           250         200          2
?NAILS             4000        4500        0.5
?HAMMERS           50          45          100
?RIVETS            5000        3000         1
?ENDFILE  0   0    0

       80 HALT
```

Having called 'CREATE' the user decides to set tabs and temporarily returns to the executive by depressing the BREAK key. Having set the tabs, he returns to BASIC and runs the program.

The last input ENDFILE 0 0 0 is not written into 'STOCK' since the program exits on detecting ENDFILE.

7·4   Program CREUP

```
10 OPEN "UPDATE" TO 2,PRINT OVER
20 N=1
30 INPUT R$,R1
40 IF R$="ENDUP" THEN 80
50 ;:2;N,R$,R1
60 N=N+1
70 GOTO 30
80 CHAIN "STKUP"
```

The user opens file 'UPDATE' and this time connects it to stream 2.

Since, after an update, he will always want to prepare a NEWSTK file his last statement automatically calls in the program STKUP which prepares the NEWSTK file.

7·5   Program STKUP

```
10 OPEN "STOCK" TO 1,INPUT
20 OPEN "UPDATE" TO 2,INPUT
30 OPEN "NEWSTK" TO 3,PRINT OVER
40 N=0
50 INPUT:1,R$,R1,R2,R3
60 N=N+1
70 ENDFILE:1,160
80 INPUT:2;1
90 INPUT:2,S$,S1
100 ENDFILE:2,140
110 IF R$<>S$ THEN 90
120 R1=R1+S1
130 GOTO 90
140 PRINT:3;N,R$,R1,R2,R3
150 GOTO 50
160 END
>
```

```
>LOAD CREUP
>RUN
09:25    OCT 20   CREUP
?NUTS              -35
?WASHERS           -66
?NUTS              -43
?ENDUP 0

     160 HALT
```

```
>LOAD FILCHK
>RUN
10:02    OCT 23   FILCHK
?NUTS
ITEM  NUTS  STOCK IS   5000
?RIVETS
ITEM  RIVETS  STOCK IS   5000
?TACKS
ITEM NOT IN STOCK
?FINISH

     130 HALT
```

The program FILRD is shown, indicating, in lines 10 and 20, one way of reading any file by changing only one statement (10).

```
10 F1="STOCK"
20 OPEN F1 TO 1,INPUT
30 INPUT:1,R$,R1,R2,R3
40 ENDFILE:1,70
50 ;R$,R1,R2,R3
60 GOTO 30
70 END
```

```
>LOAD FILRD
>RUN
09:35   OCT 20   FILRD
NUTS            5000           2500           1
WASHERS          250            200           2
NAILS           4000           4500           .500000
HAMMERS           50             45           100
RIVETS          5000           3000           1

      70 HALT
```

```
>10 F1="NEWSTK"
>RUN
09:37   OCT 20   FILRD
NUTS            4922           2500           1
WASHERS          184            200           2
NAILS           4000           4500           .500000
HAMMERS           50             45           100
RIVETS          5000           3000           1

      70 HALT
```

7·6   Program STKCPY

```
10 OPEN "NEWSTK" TO 1,INPUT
20 OPEN "STOCK" TO 2, INPUT,UPDATE
30 N=0
40 INPUT:1,R$,R1,R2,R3
50 ENDFILE:1,100
60 N=N+1
70 ;:2;N,R$,R1,R2,R3
80 GOTO40
100 END
>
```

```
>LOAD STKCPY
>RUN
14:57   OCT 23   STKCPY

      100 HALT
>LOAD FILRD
>RUN


14:58   OCT 23   FILRD
NUTS            4922           2500           1
WASHERS          184            200           2
NAILS           4000           4500           .500000
HAMMERS           50             45           100
RIVETS          5000           3000           1

      70 HALT
```

Index